**TEACHER'S PET PUBLICATIONS**

## PUZZLE PACK
for
Death of a Salesman
based on the play by
Arthur Miller

Written by
William T. Collins

© 2005 Teacher's Pet Publications
All Rights Reserved

The materials in this packet are copyrighted
by Teacher's Pet Publications, Inc.

These pages may be duplicated by the purchaser
for use in the purchaser's own classroom.

Copying any of these materials and distributing them
for any other purpose is a violation of the copyright laws.

© 2005 Teacher's Pet Publications, Inc.
www.tpet.com

## INTRODUCTION
If you already own the LitPlan for this title, this Puzzle Pack will refresh your Unit Resource Materials and Vocabulary Resource Materials sections plus give you additional materials you can substitute into the tests. If you do not already have a complete LitPlan, these pages will give you some supplemental materials to use with your own plan. There are two main groups of materials: one set for unit words (such as characters' names, symbols, places, etc.) and one set for vocabulary words associated with the book.

## WORD LIST
There is a word list for both the unit words and the vocabulary words. These lists show you which words are being used in the materials and the clues or definitions being used for those words. You may want to give students a word list with clues/definitions to help them, or you may want students to only have a word list (without clues/definitions) if you want them to work a little harder. Both are available for duplication. The word lists can also be your "calling key" for the bingo games.

## FILL IN THE BLANK AND MATCHING
There are 4 each of the fill in the blank and matching worksheets for both the unit and vocabulary words. These pages can be used either as extra worksheets for students or as objective parts of a unit test. They can be done individually if students need extra help or as a whole class activity to review the material covered.

## MAGIC SQUARES
The magic squares not only reinforce the material covered but also work on reasoning and math skills. Many teachers have told us that their students really enjoy doing these!

## WORD SEARCH PUZZLES
The word search words go in all directions, as indicated on your answer keys. Two of the word search puzzles have the clues listed rather than the words. This makes the puzzle a little more difficult, but it reinforces the material better. Two word search puzzles have words only for students who find the clue puzzles too difficult.

## CROSSWORD PUZZLES
Both unit and vocabulary word sections have 4 crossword puzzles.

## BINGO CARDS
There are 32 individual bingo cards for the unit words and 32 individual bingo cards for the vocabulary words. You can use your word list as a "call list," calling the words at random and marking them off of your list as you go, or you could use the flash cards by cutting them apart and drawing the words at random from a hat (or box or whatever). To make a better review, you might ask for the definition and spelling of each word as you call it out–or you could call out the definitions and have students tell you the words they need to look for on the puzzle.

## JUGGLE LETTERS
The vocabulary juggle letter game is intended to help students learn the spellings of the words. One sheet has the definitions listed on it as an extra help for students who need it or to reinforce the definitions if you choose to do so.

## FLASH CARDS
We've included a set of vocabulary flash cards you can duplicate, cut, and fold for your students. Some teachers make a few sets for general use by the class; others make a set for each student. Some teachers duplicate them for each student and have the students cut & fold their own. You can cut out just the words and put them in a hat, have each student pick out one word and write the definition and a sentence for that word. Students then swap words and papers, with the next student adding a sentence of his own under the last one. You can have students swap as many times as you like. Each time the student will read the sentences written prior to his own and then add a sentence. You can cut out the words and definitions separately and play "I Have; Who Has?" Each student in the room draws a word and definition. The first student says, "I have (the name of the word). Who has the definition?" The student with the definition reads it then says, "I have (the name of the vocabulary word she has). Who has the definition?" The round continues until all words and definitions have been given.

### Death of a Salesman Word List

| No. | Word | Clue/Definition |
|---|---|---|
| 1. | ANSWERS | Willy wanted Bernard to give the test ____ to Biff |
| 2. | ATTENTION | ____ must be paid to such a person |
| 3. | BEN | Willy's brother |
| 4. | BERNARD | Charley's son |
| 5. | BIFF | Willy's oldest son |
| 6. | CAR | Transportation that helped Willy in life and to death |
| 7. | CARDS | Game Charley and Willy played |
| 8. | CATTLE | Ranch animals |
| 9. | CHARLEY | He loans Willy money |
| 10. | COACH | He would probably congratulate Biff for his industriousness |
| 11. | COMMISSION | Percentage of sales as payment |
| 12. | DIAMONDS | The jungle is dark but full off ____ |
| 13. | DREAMS | He had all the wrong ____. All, all wrong. |
| 14. | ENGLAND | Willy is the New ____ Man; he can't work in NY |
| 15. | EXCUSES | What Linda makes for Willy's actions |
| 16. | FLUTES | Willy's father made and sold them |
| 17. | FOOTBALL | Biff stole one from school |
| 18. | FORSYTHE | Happy tries to pick her up at the restaurant |
| 19. | FREE | We're ____ and clear |
| 20. | FRUIT | A man isn't a piece of ____ |
| 21. | HAPPY | Willy's youngest son |
| 22. | HOWARD | He fires Willy |
| 23. | INSURANCE | Willy wants to borrow money from Charley to pay for it |
| 24. | JAILS | ____ are full of fearless characters |
| 25. | JUNGLE | Ben walked into one and came out rich |
| 26. | LIE | I realized what a ridiculous ____ my whole life has been |
| 27. | LINDA | Willy's wife |
| 28. | LOMAN | Willy's last name |
| 29. | MILLER | Author |
| 30. | MORTGAGE | Monthly house payment |
| 31. | NICKEL | When a deposit bottle is broken, you can't get your ____ back |
| 32. | OLIVER | Bill____; Biff wants money from him |
| 33. | PEN | Biff took Bill Oliver's |
| 34. | PREMIUM | Insurance payment |
| 35. | PRIDE | This is no time for false ____, Willy |
| 36. | PRINCE | Biff calls Willy a 'fine, troubled ____' |
| 37. | RANCH | Biff wants money from Bill Oliver for this |
| 38. | RESTAURANT | The boys left Willy there |
| 39. | SALESMAN | Death of a ____ |
| 40. | SEEDS | Willy wanted to plant them |
| 41. | WILLY | The salesman |
| 42. | WOMAN | Person with whom Willy has a brief affair in Boston |
| 43. | WOODS | The ____ are burning, boys. |

Death of a Salesman Fill In The Blanks 1

_____
_____
_____
_____
_____
_____
_____
_____
_____
_____
_____
_____
_____
_____
_____
_____
_____
_____
_____
_____

1. What Linda makes for Willy's actions
2. The salesman
3. Monthly house payment
4. Ben walked into one and came out rich
5. Willy's youngest son
6. Willy's last name
7. I realized what a ridiculous ____ my whole life has been
8. When a deposit bottle is broken, you can't get your ____ back
9. Transportation that helped Willy in life and to death
10. The boys left Willy there
11. Percentage of sales as payment
12. Charley's son
13. Willy is the New ____ Man; he can't work in NY
14. Insurance payment
15. Biff calls Willy a 'fine, troubled ____'
16. Willy wants to borrow money from Charley to pay for it
17. Willy's brother
18. Game Charley and Willy played
19. We're ____ and clear
20. He fires Willy

Death of a Salesman Fill In The Blanks 1 Answer Key

| | |
|---|---|
| EXCUSES | 1. What Linda makes for Willy's actions |
| WILLY | 2. The salesman |
| MORTGAGE | 3. Monthly house payment |
| JUNGLE | 4. Ben walked into one and came out rich |
| HAPPY | 5. Willy's youngest son |
| LOMAN | 6. Willy's last name |
| LIE | 7. I realized what a ridiculous ____ my whole life has been |
| NICKEL | 8. When a deposit bottle is broken, you can't get your ____ back |
| CAR | 9. Transportation that helped Willy in life and to death |
| RESTAURANT | 10. The boys left Willy there |
| COMMISSION | 11. Percentage of sales as payment |
| BERNARD | 12. Charley's son |
| ENGLAND | 13. Willy is the New ____ Man; he can't work in NY |
| PREMIUM | 14. Insurance payment |
| PRINCE | 15. Biff calls Willy a 'fine, troubled ____' |
| INSURANCE | 16. Willy wants to borrow money from Charley to pay for it |
| BEN | 17. Willy's brother |
| CARDS | 18. Game Charley and Willy played |
| FREE | 19. We're ____ and clear |
| HOWARD | 20. He fires Willy |

Death of a Salesman Fill In The Blanks 2

_____  1. Willy's oldest son

_____  2. He loans Willy money

_____  3. He would probably congratulate Biff for his industriousness

_____  4. Biff stole one from school

_____  5. Happy tries to pick her up at the restaurant

_____  6. Author

_____  7. When a deposit bottle is broken, you can't get your ____ back

_____  8. He fires Willy

_____  9. Willy wanted Bernard to give the test ____ to Biff

_____  10. ____ must be paid to such a person

_____  11. Ben walked into one and came out rich

_____  12. Bill____; Biff wants money from him

_____  13. Biff calls Willy a 'fine, troubled ____'

_____  14. Monthly house payment

_____  15. Insurance payment

_____  16. Person with whom Willy has a brief affair in Boston

_____  17. Biff wants money from Bill Oliver for this

_____  18. Transportation that helped Willy in life and to death

_____  19. The ____ are burning, boys.

_____  20. Willy's last name

Death of a Salesman Fill In The Blanks 2 Answer Key

| | |
|---|---|
| BIFF | 1. Willy's oldest son |
| CHARLEY | 2. He loans Willy money |
| COACH | 3. He would probably congratulate Biff for his industriousness |
| FOOTBALL | 4. Biff stole one from school |
| FORSYTHE | 5. Happy tries to pick her up at the restaurant |
| MILLER | 6. Author |
| NICKEL | 7. When a deposit bottle is broken, you can't get your ____ back |
| HOWARD | 8. He fires Willy |
| ANSWERS | 9. Willy wanted Bernard to give the test ____ to Biff |
| ATTENTION | 10. ____ must be paid to such a person |
| JUNGLE | 11. Ben walked into one and came out rich |
| OLIVER | 12. Bill____; Biff wants money from him |
| PRINCE | 13. Biff calls Willy a 'fine, troubled ____' |
| MORTGAGE | 14. Monthly house payment |
| PREMIUM | 15. Insurance payment |
| WOMAN | 16. Person with whom Willy has a brief affair in Boston |
| RANCH | 17. Biff wants money from Bill Oliver for this |
| CAR | 18. Transportation that helped Willy in life and to death |
| WOODS | 19. The ____ are burning, boys. |
| LOMAN | 20. Willy's last name |

Copyrighted

Death of a Salesman Fill In The Blanks 3

_____

_____

_____

_____

_____

_____

_____

_____

_____

_____

_____

_____

_____

_____

_____

_____

_____

_____

_____

_____

1. Transportation that helped Willy in life and to death
2. ____ are full of fearless characters
3. Person with whom Willy has a brief affair in Boston
4. Willy's brother
5. The salesman
6. Happy tries to pick her up at the restaurant
7. Bill____; Biff wants money from him
8. Biff took Bill Oliver's
9. Willy's youngest son
10. The boys left Willy there
11. Willy's wife
12. Willy is the New ____ Man; he can't work in NY
13. Willy wanted Bernard to give the test ____ to Biff
14. Willy's father made and sold them
15. Death of a ____
16. What Linda makes for Willy's actions
17. He had all the wrong ____. All, all wrong.
18. Charley's son
19. He loans Willy money
20. A man isn't a piece of ____

Death of a Salesman Fill In The Blanks 3 Answer Key

|  |  |
|---|---|
| CAR | 1. Transportation that helped Willy in life and to death |
| JAILS | 2. ____ are full of fearless characters |
| WOMAN | 3. Person with whom Willy has a brief affair in Boston |
| BEN | 4. Willy's brother |
| WILLY | 5. The salesman |
| FORSYTHE | 6. Happy tries to pick her up at the restaurant |
| OLIVER | 7. Bill____; Biff wants money from him |
| PEN | 8. Biff took Bill Oliver's |
| HAPPY | 9. Willy's youngest son |
| RESTAURANT | 10. The boys left Willy there |
| LINDA | 11. Willy's wife |
| ENGLAND | 12. Willy is the New ____ Man; he can't work in NY |
| ANSWERS | 13. Willy wanted Bernard to give the test ____ to Biff |
| FLUTES | 14. Willy's father made and sold them |
| SALESMAN | 15. Death of a ____ |
| EXCUSES | 16. What Linda makes for Willy's actions |
| DREAMS | 17. He had all the wrong ____. All, all wrong. |
| BERNARD | 18. Charley's son |
| CHARLEY | 19. He loans Willy money |
| FRUIT | 20. A man isn't a piece of ____ |

Death of a Salesman Fill In The Blanks 4

1. The boys left Willy there
2. He had all the wrong _____. All, all wrong.
3. Willy's father made and sold them
4. He would probably congratulate Biff for his industriousness
5. Charley's son
6. Insurance payment
7. Person with whom Willy has a brief affair in Boston
8. Willy's youngest son
9. Willy's brother
10. Biff stole one from school
11. A man isn't a piece of _____
12. Percentage of sales as payment
13. Transportation that helped Willy in life and to death
14. _____ are full of fearless characters
15. When a deposit bottle is broken, you can't get your _____ back
16. _____ must be paid to such a person
17. Monthly house payment
18. He fires Willy
19. Willy wanted Bernard to give the test _____ to Biff
20. What Linda makes for Willy's actions

Death of a Salesman Fill In The Blanks 4 Answer Key

| | |
|---|---|
| RESTAURANT | 1. The boys left Willy there |
| DREAMS | 2. He had all the wrong ____. All, all wrong. |
| FLUTES | 3. Willy's father made and sold them |
| COACH | 4. He would probably congratulate Biff for his industriousness |
| BERNARD | 5. Charley's son |
| PREMIUM | 6. Insurance payment |
| WOMAN | 7. Person with whom Willy has a brief affair in Boston |
| HAPPY | 8. Willy's youngest son |
| BEN | 9. Willy's brother |
| FOOTBALL | 10. Biff stole one from school |
| FRUIT | 11. A man isn't a piece of ____ |
| COMMISSION | 12. Percentage of sales as payment |
| CAR | 13. Transportation that helped Willy in life and to death |
| JAILS | 14. ____ are full of fearless characters |
| NICKEL | 15. When a deposit bottle is broken, you can't get your ____ back |
| ATTENTION | 16. ____ must be paid to such a person |
| MORTGAGE | 17. Monthly house payment |
| HOWARD | 18. He fires Willy |
| ANSWERS | 19. Willy wanted Bernard to give the test ____ to Biff |
| EXCUSES | 20. What Linda makes for Willy's actions |

Death of a Salesman Matching 1

___ 1. FORSYTHE
___ 2. SALESMAN
___ 3. BEN
___ 4. INSURANCE
___ 5. BERNARD
___ 6. NICKEL
___ 7. FOOTBALL
___ 8. JUNGLE
___ 9. WOMAN
___ 10. ANSWERS
___ 11. WOODS
___ 12. PEN
___ 13. PRINCE
___ 14. SEEDS
___ 15. LINDA
___ 16. JAILS
___ 17. MORTGAGE
___ 18. WILLY
___ 19. FRUIT
___ 20. CHARLEY
___ 21. COMMISSION
___ 22. DREAMS
___ 23. EXCUSES
___ 24. LIE
___ 25. RANCH

A. Willy wants to borrow money from Charley to pay for it
B. Biff calls Willy a 'fine, troubled ____'
C. Monthly house payment
D. When a deposit bottle is broken, you can't get your ____ back
E. I realized what a ridiculous ____ my whole life has been
F. Happy tries to pick her up at the restaurant
G. He loans Willy money
H. Biff stole one from school
I. Percentage of sales as payment
J. Willy's wife
K. Willy wanted to plant them
L. Person with whom Willy has a brief affair in Boston
M. Willy's brother
N. He had all the wrong ____. All, all wrong.
O. What Linda makes for Willy's actions
P. Death of a ____
Q. A man isn't a piece of ____
R. The salesman
S. Willy wanted Bernard to give the test ____ to Biff
T. Biff wants money from Bill Oliver for this
U. The ____ are burning, boys.
V. Charley's son
W. Ben walked into one and came out rich
X. ____ are full of fearless characters
Y. Biff took Bill Oliver's

Death of a Salesman Matching 1 Answer Key

| | | |
|---|---|---|
| F - 1. FORSYTHE | | A. Willy wants to borrow money from Charley to pay for it |
| P - 2. SALESMAN | | B. Biff calls Willy a 'fine, troubled ____' |
| M - 3. BEN | | C. Monthly house payment |
| A - 4. INSURANCE | | D. When a deposit bottle is broken, you can't get your ____ back |
| V - 5. BERNARD | | E. I realized what a ridiculous ____ my whole life has been |
| D - 6. NICKEL | | F. Happy tries to pick her up at the restaurant |
| H - 7. FOOTBALL | | G. He loans Willy money |
| W - 8. JUNGLE | | H. Biff stole one from school |
| L - 9. WOMAN | | I. Percentage of sales as payment |
| S - 10. ANSWERS | | J. Willy's wife |
| U - 11. WOODS | | K. Willy wanted to plant them |
| Y - 12. PEN | | L. Person with whom Willy has a brief affair in Boston |
| B - 13. PRINCE | | M. Willy's brother |
| K - 14. SEEDS | | N. He had all the wrong ____. All, all wrong. |
| J - 15. LINDA | | O. What Linda makes for Willy's actions |
| X - 16. JAILS | | P. Death of a ____ |
| C - 17. MORTGAGE | | Q. A man isn't a piece of ____ |
| R - 18. WILLY | | R. The salesman |
| Q - 19. FRUIT | | S. Willy wanted Bernard to give the test ____ to Biff |
| G - 20. CHARLEY | | T. Biff wants money from Bill Oliver for this |
| I - 21. COMMISSION | | U. The ____ are burning, boys. |
| N - 22. DREAMS | | V. Charley's son |
| O - 23. EXCUSES | | W. Ben walked into one and came out rich |
| E - 24. LIE | | X. ____ are full of fearless characters |
| T - 25. RANCH | | Y. Biff took Bill Oliver's |

Death of a Salesman Matching 2

___ 1. COACH           A. He had all the wrong ____. All, all wrong.
___ 2. CATTLE          B. ____ must be paid to such a person
___ 3. WILLY           C. A man isn't a piece of ____
___ 4. MILLER          D. What Linda makes for Willy's actions
___ 5. BERNARD         E. He loans Willy money
___ 6. EXCUSES         F. Willy wants to borrow money from Charley to pay for it
___ 7. CHARLEY         G. The ____ are burning, boys.
___ 8. HAPPY           H. He would probably congratulate Biff for his industriousness
___ 9. CAR             I. Bill____; Biff wants money from him
___10. ATTENTION       J. Charley's son
___11. LINDA           K. Biff wants money from Bill Oliver for this
___12. HOWARD          L. The jungle is dark but full off ____
___13. DREAMS          M. We're ____ and clear
___14. INSURANCE       N. Biff stole one from school
___15. WOODS           O. Willy's youngest son
___16. FREE            P. He fires Willy
___17. OLIVER          Q. Author
___18. FOOTBALL        R. Transportation that helped Willy in life and to death
___19. PREMIUM         S. Willy's wife
___20. DIAMONDS        T. Person with whom Willy has a brief affair in Boston
___21. FRUIT           U. Insurance payment
___22. JUNGLE          V. The salesman
___23. WOMAN           W. Ben walked into one and came out rich
___24. RESTAURANT      X. The boys left Willy there
___25. RANCH           Y. Ranch animals

Death of a Salesman Matching 2 Answer Key

H - 1. COACH
Y - 2. CATTLE
V - 3. WILLY
Q - 4. MILLER
J - 5. BERNARD
D - 6. EXCUSES
E - 7. CHARLEY
O - 8. HAPPY
R - 9. CAR
B - 10. ATTENTION
S - 11. LINDA
P - 12. HOWARD
A - 13. DREAMS
F - 14. INSURANCE
G - 15. WOODS
M - 16. FREE
I - 17. OLIVER
N - 18. FOOTBALL
U - 19. PREMIUM
L - 20. DIAMONDS
C - 21. FRUIT
W - 22. JUNGLE
T - 23. WOMAN
X - 24. RESTAURANT
K - 25. RANCH

A. He had all the wrong ____. All, all wrong.
B. ____ must be paid to such a person
C. A man isn't a piece of ____
D. What Linda makes for Willy's actions
E. He loans Willy money
F. Willy wants to borrow money from Charley to pay for it
G. The ____ are burning, boys.
H. He would probably congratulate Biff for his industriousness
I. Bill____; Biff wants money from him
J. Charley's son
K. Biff wants money from Bill Oliver for this
L. The jungle is dark but full off ____
M. We're ____ and clear
N. Biff stole one from school
O. Willy's youngest son
P. He fires Willy
Q. Author
R. Transportation that helped Willy in life and to death
S. Willy's wife
T. Person with whom Willy has a brief affair in Boston
U. Insurance payment
V. The salesman
W. Ben walked into one and came out rich
X. The boys left Willy there
Y. Ranch animals

Death of a Salesman Matching 3

___ 1. COMMISSION  A. Willy's brother
___ 2. PREMIUM  B. Biff stole one from school
___ 3. DREAMS  C. Insurance payment
___ 4. LIE  D. Willy wants to borrow money from Charley to pay for it
___ 5. ENGLAND  E. When a deposit bottle is broken, you can't get your ____ back
___ 6. NICKEL  F. Charley's son
___ 7. FLUTES  G. Willy is the New ____ Man; he can't work in NY
___ 8. BEN  H. Percentage of sales as payment
___ 9. RANCH  I. Ben walked into one and came out rich
___ 10. ATTENTION  J. I realized what a ridiculous ____ my whole life has been
___ 11. FOOTBALL  K. Willy's oldest son
___ 12. JUNGLE  L. Biff wants money from Bill Oliver for this
___ 13. FREE  M. Happy tries to pick her up at the restaurant
___ 14. CAR  N. Ranch animals
___ 15. MILLER  O. The salesman
___ 16. BERNARD  P. Author
___ 17. BIFF  Q. Willy's wife
___ 18. LINDA  R. Willy wanted Bernard to give the test ____ to Biff
___ 19. CATTLE  S. Transportation that helped Willy in life and to death
___ 20. FORSYTHE  T. He had all the wrong ____. All, all wrong.
___ 21. WILLY  U. He would probably congratulate Biff for his industriousness
___ 22. ANSWERS  V. ____ must be paid to such a person
___ 23. FRUIT  W. A man isn't a piece of ____
___ 24. COACH  X. Willy's father made and sold them
___ 25. INSURANCE  Y. We're ____ and clear

Death of a Salesman Matching 3 Answer Key

H - 1. COMMISSION    A. Willy's brother
C - 2. PREMIUM       B. Biff stole one from school
T - 3. DREAMS        C. Insurance payment
J - 4. LIE           D. Willy wants to borrow money from Charley to pay for it
G - 5. ENGLAND       E. When a deposit bottle is broken, you can't get your ____ back
E - 6. NICKEL        F. Charley's son
X - 7. FLUTES        G. Willy is the New ____ Man; he can't work in NY
A - 8. BEN           H. Percentage of sales as payment
L - 9. RANCH         I. Ben walked into one and came out rich
V - 10. ATTENTION    J. I realized what a ridiculous ____ my whole life has been
B - 11. FOOTBALL     K. Willy's oldest son
I - 12. JUNGLE       L. Biff wants money from Bill Oliver for this
Y - 13. FREE         M. Happy tries to pick her up at the restaurant
S - 14. CAR          N. Ranch animals
P - 15. MILLER       O. The salesman
F - 16. BERNARD      P. Author
K - 17. BIFF         Q. Willy's wife
Q - 18. LINDA        R. Willy wanted Bernard to give the test ____ to Biff
N - 19. CATTLE       S. Transportation that helped Willy in life and to death
M - 20. FORSYTHE     T. He had all the wrong ____. All, all wrong.
O - 21. WILLY        U. He would probably congratulate Biff for his industriousness
R - 22. ANSWERS      V. ____ must be paid to such a person
W - 23. FRUIT        W. A man isn't a piece of ____
U - 24. COACH        X. Willy's father made and sold them
D - 25. INSURANCE    Y. We're ____ and clear

Death of a Salesman Matching 4

___ 1. MORTGAGE  A. Author
___ 2. PRINCE  B. Willy's oldest son
___ 3. FRUIT  C. Biff stole one from school
___ 4. BERNARD  D. Death of a ____
___ 5. HOWARD  E. Charley's son
___ 6. MILLER  F. Bill____; Biff wants money from him
___ 7. ATTENTION  G. The boys left Willy there
___ 8. COACH  H. A man isn't a piece of ____
___ 9. FOOTBALL  I. ____ must be paid to such a person
___10. OLIVER  J. Monthly house payment
___11. SALESMAN  K. Ranch animals
___12. CATTLE  L. Insurance payment
___13. JUNGLE  M. Willy's father made and sold them
___14. LINDA  N. Biff wants money from Bill Oliver for this
___15. INSURANCE  O. He loans Willy money
___16. BIFF  P. Willy wanted to plant them
___17. COMMISSION  Q. He would probably congratulate Biff for his industriousness
___18. RANCH  R. Willy's brother
___19. FLUTES  S. He fires Willy
___20. CHARLEY  T. Biff calls Willy a 'fine, troubled ____'
___21. BEN  U. Transportation that helped Willy in life and to death
___22. RESTAURANT  V. Percentage of sales as payment
___23. SEEDS  W. Ben walked into one and came out rich
___24. CAR  X. Willy wants to borrow money from Charley to pay for it
___25. PREMIUM  Y. Willy's wife

Death of a Salesman Matching 4 Answer Key

J - 1. MORTGAGE
T - 2. PRINCE
H - 3. FRUIT
E - 4. BERNARD
S - 5. HOWARD
A - 6. MILLER
I - 7. ATTENTION
Q - 8. COACH
C - 9. FOOTBALL
F - 10. OLIVER
D - 11. SALESMAN
K - 12. CATTLE
W - 13. JUNGLE
Y - 14. LINDA
X - 15. INSURANCE
B - 16. BIFF
V - 17. COMMISSION
N - 18. RANCH
M - 19. FLUTES
O - 20. CHARLEY
R - 21. BEN
G - 22. RESTAURANT
P - 23. SEEDS
U - 24. CAR
L - 25. PREMIUM

A. Author
B. Willy's oldest son
C. Biff stole one from school
D. Death of a ____
E. Charley's son
F. Bill____; Biff wants money from him
G. The boys left Willy there
H. A man isn't a piece of ____
I. ____ must be paid to such a person
J. Monthly house payment
K. Ranch animals
L. Insurance payment
M. Willy's father made and sold them
N. Biff wants money from Bill Oliver for this
O. He loans Willy money
P. Willy wanted to plant them
Q. He would probably congratulate Biff for his industriousness
R. Willy's brother
S. He fires Willy
T. Biff calls Willy a 'fine, troubled ____'
U. Transportation that helped Willy in life and to death
V. Percentage of sales as payment
W. Ben walked into one and came out rich
X. Willy wants to borrow money from Charley to pay for it
Y. Willy's wife

Death of a Salesman Magic Squares 1

Match the definition with the vocabulary word. Put your answers in the magic squares below. When your answers are correct, all columns and rows will add to the same number.

A. FREE
B. CAR
C. HAPPY
D. ANSWERS
E. FORSYTHE
F. COACH
G. WOMAN
H. EXCUSES
I. PRINCE
J. FOOTBALL
K. RESTAURANT
L. JAILS
M. JUNGLE
N. PRIDE
O. LOMAN
P. RANCH

1. This is no time for false ____, Willy
2. Person with whom Willy has a brief affair in Boston
3. ____ are full of fearless characters
4. We're ____ and clear
5. The boys left Willy there
6. Transportation that helped Willy in life and to death
7. Ben walked into one and came out rich
8. What Linda makes for Willy's actions
9. Happy tries to pick her up at the restaurant
10. Biff wants money from Bill Oliver for this
11. Willy's youngest son
12. Biff stole one from school
13. Willy wanted Bernard to give the test ____ to Biff
14. Biff calls Willy a 'fine, troubled ____'
15. He would probably congratulate Biff for his industriousness
16. Willy's last name

| A= | B= | C= | D= |
| --- | --- | --- | --- |
| E= | F= | G= | H= |
| I= | J= | K= | L= |
| M= | N= | O= | P= |

Death of a Salesman Magic Squares 1 Answer Key

Match the definition with the vocabulary word. Put your answers in the magic squares below. When your answers are correct, all columns and rows will add to the same number.

A. FREE
B. CAR
C. HAPPY
D. ANSWERS
E. FORSYTHE
F. COACH
G. WOMAN
H. EXCUSES
I. PRINCE
J. FOOTBALL
K. RESTAURANT
L. JAILS
M. JUNGLE
N. PRIDE
O. LOMAN
P. RANCH

1. This is no time for false ____, Willy
2. Person with whom Willy has a brief affair in Boston
3. ____ are full of fearless characters
4. We're ____ and clear
5. The boys left Willy there
6. Transportation that helped Willy in life and to death
7. Ben walked into one and came out rich
8. What Linda makes for Willy's actions
9. Happy tries to pick her up at the restaurant
10. Biff wants money from Bill Oliver for this
11. Willy's youngest son
12. Biff stole one from school
13. Willy wanted Bernard to give the test ____ to Biff
14. Biff calls Willy a 'fine, troubled ____'
15. He would probably congratulate Biff for his industriousness
16. Willy's last name

| A=4 | B=6 | C=11 | D=13 |
| --- | --- | --- | --- |
| E=9 | F=15 | G=2 | H=8 |
| I=14 | J=12 | K=5 | L=3 |
| M=7 | N=1 | O=16 | P=10 |

Death of a Salesman Magic Squares 2

Match the definition with the vocabulary word. Put your answers in the magic squares below. When your answers are correct, all columns and rows will add to the same number.

A. HOWARD
B. FLUTES
C. JUNGLE
D. MORTGAGE
E. SALESMAN
F. BEN
G. WILLY
H. PREMIUM
I. CATTLE
J. ENGLAND
K. DIAMONDS
L. HAPPY
M. PEN
N. INSURANCE
O. NICKEL
P. WOMAN

1. Willy's brother
2. Ranch animals
3. When a deposit bottle is broken, you can't get your ____ back
4. Monthly house payment
5. Biff took Bill Oliver's
6. Willy's father made and sold them
7. Insurance payment
8. The jungle is dark but full off ____
9. Ben walked into one and came out rich
10. Person with whom Willy has a brief affair in Boston
11. Willy is the New ____ Man; he can't work in NY
12. Death of a ____
13. Willy's youngest son
14. The salesman
15. He fires Willy
16. Willy wants to borrow money from Charley to pay for it

| A= | B= | C= | D= |
| E= | F= | G= | H= |
| I= | J= | K= | L= |
| M= | N= | O= | P= |

Death of a Salesman Magic Squares 2 Answer Key

Match the definition with the vocabulary word. Put your answers in the magic squares below. When your answers are correct, all columns and rows will add to the same number.

A. HOWARD
B. FLUTES
C. JUNGLE
D. MORTGAGE
E. SALESMAN
F. BEN

G. WILLY
H. PREMIUM
I. CATTLE
J. ENGLAND
K. DIAMONDS
L. HAPPY

M. PEN
N. INSURANCE
O. NICKEL
P. WOMAN

1. Willy's brother
2. Ranch animals
3. When a deposit bottle is broken, you can't get your ____ back
4. Monthly house payment
5. Biff took Bill Oliver's
6. Willy's father made and sold them
7. Insurance payment
8. The jungle is dark but full off ____
9. Ben walked into one and came out rich
10. Person with whom Willy has a brief affair in Boston
11. Willy is the New ____ Man; he can't work in NY
12. Death of a ____
13. Willy's youngest son
14. The salesman
15. He fires Willy
16. Willy wants to borrow money from Charley to pay for it

| A=15 | B=6 | C=9 | D=4 |
|---|---|---|---|
| E=12 | F=1 | G=14 | H=7 |
| I=2 | J=11 | K=8 | L=13 |
| M=5 | N=16 | O=3 | P=10 |

Death of a Salesman Magic Squares 3

Match the definition with the vocabulary word. Put your answers in the magic squares below. When your answers are correct, all columns and rows will add to the same number.

A. BEN
B. JUNGLE
C. RESTAURANT
D. CATTLE
E. MORTGAGE
F. RANCH
G. JAILS
H. CARDS
I. FREE
J. FOOTBALL
K. LIE
L. ATTENTION
M. DREAMS
N. EXCUSES
O. PREMIUM
P. WILLY

1. Ben walked into one and came out rich
2. ____ are full of fearless characters
3. I realized what a ridiculous ____ my whole life has been
4. What Linda makes for Willy's actions
5. He had all the wrong ____. All, all wrong.
6. ____ must be paid to such a person
7. Game Charley and Willy played
8. Willy's brother
9. The salesman
10. We're ____ and clear
11. Monthly house payment
12. Ranch animals
13. The boys left Willy there
14. Biff wants money from Bill Oliver for this
15. Biff stole one from school
16. Insurance payment

| A= | B= | C= | D= |
|---|---|---|---|
| E= | F= | G= | H= |
| I= | J= | K= | L= |
| M= | N= | O= | P= |

Death of a Salesman Magic Squares 3 Answer Key

Match the definition with the vocabulary word. Put your answers in the magic squares below. When your answers are correct, all columns and rows will add to the same number.

A. BEN
B. JUNGLE
C. RESTAURANT
D. CATTLE
E. MORTGAGE
F. RANCH
G. JAILS
H. CARDS
I. FREE
J. FOOTBALL
K. LIE
L. ATTENTION
M. DREAMS
N. EXCUSES
O. PREMIUM
P. WILLY

1. Ben walked into one and came out rich
2. ____ are full of fearless characters
3. I realized what a ridiculous ____ my whole life has been
4. What Linda makes for Willy's actions
5. He had all the wrong ____. All, all wrong.
6. ____ must be paid to such a person
7. Game Charley and Willy played
8. Willy's brother
9. The salesman
10. We're ____ and clear
11. Monthly house payment
12. Ranch animals
13. The boys left Willy there
14. Biff wants money from Bill Oliver for this
15. Biff stole one from school
16. Insurance payment

| A=8 | B=1 | C=13 | D=12 |
| --- | --- | --- | --- |
| E=11 | F=14 | G=2 | H=7 |
| I=10 | J=15 | K=3 | L=6 |
| M=5 | N=4 | O=16 | P=9 |

Death of a Salesman Magic Squares 4

Match the definition with the vocabulary word. Put your answers in the magic squares below. When your answers are correct, all columns and rows will add to the same number.

A. RESTAURANT
B. SALESMAN
C. FORSYTHE
D. CATTLE
E. CARDS
F. LOMAN
G. HAPPY
H. MILLER
I. COMMISSION
J. BIFF
K. WILLY
L. NICKEL
M. INSURANCE
N. FRUIT
O. DIAMONDS
P. BERNARD

1. The boys left Willy there
2. A man isn't a piece of ____
3. Willy's oldest son
4. Game Charley and Willy played
5. Willy's youngest son
6. When a deposit bottle is broken, you can't get your ____ back
7. Charley's son
8. Happy tries to pick her up at the restaurant
9. The jungle is dark but full off ____
10. Ranch animals
11. Author
12. The salesman
13. Percentage of sales as payment
14. Willy's last name
15. Death of a ____
16. Willy wants to borrow money from Charley to pay for it

| A= | B= | C= | D= |
| --- | --- | --- | --- |
| E= | F= | G= | H= |
| I= | J= | K= | L= |
| M= | N= | O= | P= |

Death of a Salesman Magic Squares 4 Answer Key

Match the definition with the vocabulary word. Put your answers in the magic squares below. When your answers are correct, all columns and rows will add to the same number.

A. RESTAURANT
B. SALESMAN
C. FORSYTHE
D. CATTLE
E. CARDS
F. LOMAN
G. HAPPY
H. MILLER
I. COMMISSION
J. BIFF
K. WILLY
L. NICKEL
M. INSURANCE
N. FRUIT
O. DIAMONDS
P. BERNARD

1. The boys left Willy there
2. A man isn't a piece of ____
3. Willy's oldest son
4. Game Charley and Willy played
5. Willy's youngest son
6. When a deposit bottle is broken, you can't get your ____ back
7. Charley's son
8. Happy tries to pick her up at the restaurant
9. The jungle is dark but full off ____
10. Ranch animals
11. Author
12. The salesman
13. Percentage of sales as payment
14. Willy's last name
15. Death of a ____
16. Willy wants to borrow money from Charley to pay for it

| A=1 | B=15 | C=8 | D=10 |
|---|---|---|---|
| E=4 | F=14 | G=5 | H=11 |
| I=13 | J=3 | K=12 | L=6 |
| M=16 | N=2 | O=9 | P=7 |

Death of a Salesman Word Search 1

Words are placed backwards, forward, diagonally, up and down. Clues listed below can help you find the words. Circle the hidden vocabulary words in the maze.

```
Z Q R F L U T E S S R E W S N A Z F N
J N Q E G A G T R O M X C F S N C O C
A J T H S P D V L Z K C S G A W L R B
I L D F Y T R K Y G B U Q M G O T S Q
L W I R N V A I C Y C S S R G M N Y G
S S D E E S J U N G L E L T T A C T D
K V B E N A W L R C L S Z I M N F H Q
Q M R W G Q M Z J A E C U O N Z D E C
X F F J L G V S S T N R L K G D R H R
V S R F A P R I D E F T W H O W A R D
W A F C N R E I T L D F I J V R N A D
C I K M D E A N R V N T L M L C R N L
B X V T C M Y M Z K X B L E X A E C F
Z T P W O I G B I L D K Y S L R B H S
W Z X N A U M B O L F H J M C D C Y B
H O D J C M S P L B L L B N T S Y H X
Z S O J H G N O I T N E T T A P G S H
D F G D P D W Q V X R L R B P F D F M
Q N F J S P W B E D E C N A R U S N I
F O O T B A L L R H J M H N I C K E L
```

A man isn't a piece of ____ (5)
Author (6)
Ben walked into one and came out rich (6)
Biff calls Willy a 'fine, troubled ____' (6)
Biff stole one from school (8)
Biff took Bill Oliver's (3)
Biff wants money from Bill Oliver for this (5)
Bill____; Biff wants money from him (6)
Charley's son (7)
Death of a ____ (8)
Game Charley and Willy played (5)
Happy tries to pick her up at the restaurant (8)
He fires Willy (6)
He had all the wrong ____. All, all wrong. (6)
He loans Willy money (7)
He would probably congratulate Biff for his industriousness (5)
I realized what a ridiculous ____ my whole life has been (3)
Insurance payment (7)
Monthly house payment (8)
Person with whom Willy has a brief affair in Boston (5)
Ranch animals (6)
The ____ are burning, boys. (5)

The boys left Willy there (10)
The jungle is dark but full off ____ (8)
The salesman (5)
This is no time for false ____, Willy (5)
Transportation that helped Willy in life and to death (3)
We're ____ and clear (4)
What Linda makes for Willy's actions (7)
When a deposit bottle is broken, you can't get your ____ back (6)
Willy is the New ____ Man; he can't work in NY (7)
Willy wanted Bernard to give the test ____ to Biff (7)
Willy wanted to plant them (5)
Willy wants to borrow money from Charley to pay for it (9)
Willy's brother (3)
Willy's father made and sold them (6)
Willy's last name (5)
Willy's oldest son (4)
Willy's wife (5)
Willy's youngest son (5)
____ are full of fearless characters (5)
____ must be paid to such a person (9)

Death of a Salesman Word Search 1 Answer Key

Words are placed backwards, forward, diagonally, up and down. Clues listed below can help you find the words. Circle the hidden vocabulary words in the maze.

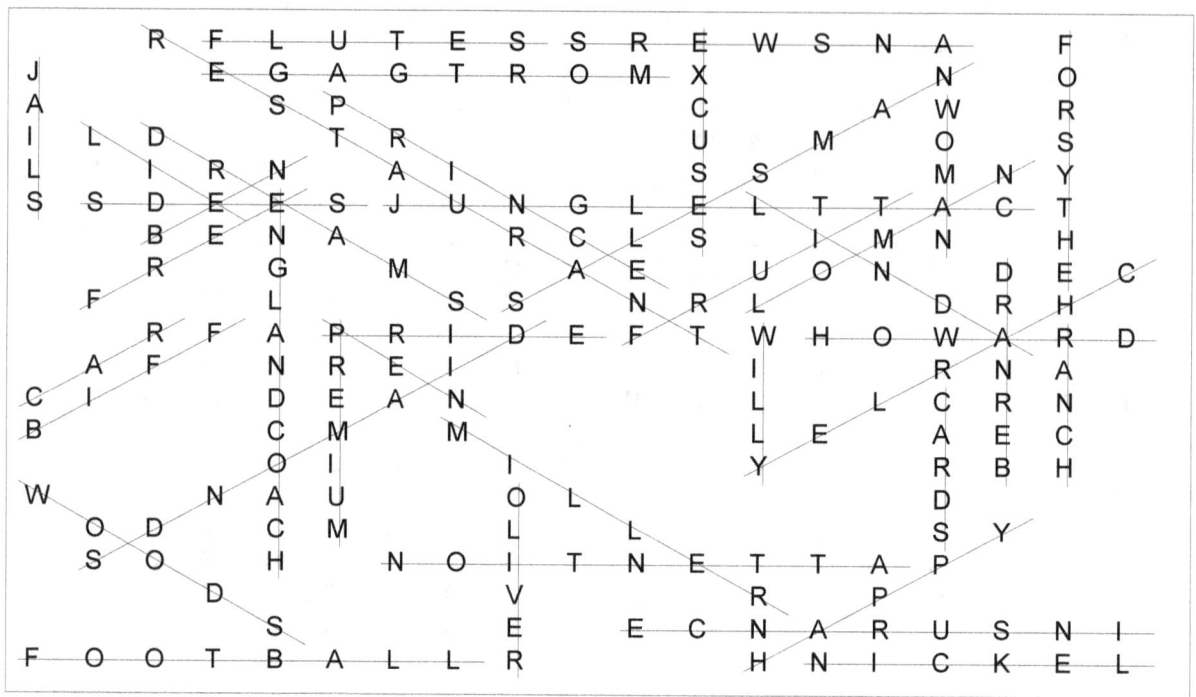

A man isn't a piece of ____ (5)
Author (6)
Ben walked into one and came out rich (6)
Biff calls Willy a 'fine, troubled ____' (6)
Biff stole one from school (8)
Biff took Bill Oliver's (3)
Biff wants money from Bill Oliver for this (5)
Bill____; Biff wants money from him (6)
Charley's son (7)
Death of a ____ (8)
Game Charley and Willy played (5)
Happy tries to pick her up at the restaurant (8)
He fires Willy (6)
He had all the wrong ____. All, all wrong. (6)
He loans Willy money (7)
He would probably congratulate Biff for his industriousness (5)
I realized what a ridiculous ____ my whole life has been (3)
Insurance payment (7)
Monthly house payment (8)
Person with whom Willy has a brief affair in Boston (5)
Ranch animals (6)
The ____ are burning, boys. (5)

The boys left Willy there (10)
The jungle is dark but full off ____ (8)
The salesman (5)
This is no time for false ____, Willy (5)
Transportation that helped Willy in life and to death (3)
We're ____ and clear (4)
What Linda makes for Willy's actions (7)
When a deposit bottle is broken, you can't get your ____ back (6)
Willy is the New ____ Man; he can't work in NY (7)
Willy wanted Bernard to give the test ____ to Biff (7)
Willy wanted to plant them (5)
Willy wants to borrow money from Charley to pay for it (9)
Willy's brother (3)
Willy's father made and sold them (6)
Willy's last name (5)
Willy's oldest son (4)
Willy's wife (5)
Willy's youngest son (5)
____ are full of fearless characters (5)
____ must be paid to such a person (9)

Death of a Salesman Word Search 2

Words are placed backwards, forward, diagonally, up and down. Clues listed below can help you find the words. Circle the hidden vocabulary words in the maze.

```
W J B E J A I L S W S A L E S M A N N
I U F X D K N N Z N O E Q W V F R F Y
L N B C L P R M S W I M E P W O A R G
L G M U I M E R P U E C A D T O N E S
Y L Y S N G Y C S L R H K N S T C E J
M E V E D L B J T J J A A E Q B H P R
G G T S A P O T W L D R N E L A R B J
F L U T E S A M W R U L Z C R L T M N
B J V B C C T H A A J E C N E L P K V
S I D W H N C W T N D Y M I L J Z C D
S K F T C A O S D O O W T R L B F N C
E V A F O H E Y V T R I S P I J Q S M
H P T C B R Y K G J U T D V M S H S W
T K T S K E N J E R W K R R L Z D C G
Y G E Y P Q R F F N R R Y K E N P A S
S S N N E C W N C D G L P Y O A M R Y
R H T D S A T J A V G L P M P Z M D D
O L I V E R W M O R T G A G E C L S D
F R O H K J Q M V K D I H N N L I F K
P A N S W E R S T L D B E N D M E F F
```

A man isn't a piece of ____ (5)
Author (6)
Ben walked into one and came out rich (6)
Biff calls Willy a 'fine, troubled ____' (6)
Biff stole one from school (8)
Biff took Bill Oliver's (3)
Biff wants money from Bill Oliver for this (5)
Bill____; Biff wants money from him (6)
Charley's son (7)
Death of a ____ (8)
Game Charley and Willy played (5)
Happy tries to pick her up at the restaurant (8)
He fires Willy (6)
He had all the wrong ____. All, all wrong. (6)
He loans Willy money (7)
He would probably congratulate Biff for his industriousness (5)
I realized what a ridiculous ____ my whole life has been (3)
Insurance payment (7)
Monthly house payment (8)
Person with whom Willy has a brief affair in Boston (5)
Ranch animals (6)
The ____ are burning, boys. (5)

The boys left Willy there (10)
The jungle is dark but full off ____ (8)
The salesman (5)
This is no time for false ____, Willy (5)
Transportation that helped Willy in life and to death (3)
We're ____ and clear (4)
What Linda makes for Willy's actions (7)
When a deposit bottle is broken, you can't get your ____ back (6)
Willy is the New ____ Man; he can't work in NY (7)
Willy wanted Bernard to give the test ____ to Biff (7)
Willy wanted to plant them (5)
Willy wants to borrow money from Charley to pay for it (9)
Willy's brother (3)
Willy's father made and sold them (6)
Willy's last name (5)
Willy's oldest son (4)
Willy's wife (5)
Willy's youngest son (5)
____ are full of fearless characters (5)
____ must be paid to such a person (9)

Death of a Salesman Word Search 2 Answer Key

Words are placed backwards, forward, diagonally, up and down. Clues listed below can help you find the words. Circle the hidden vocabulary words in the maze.

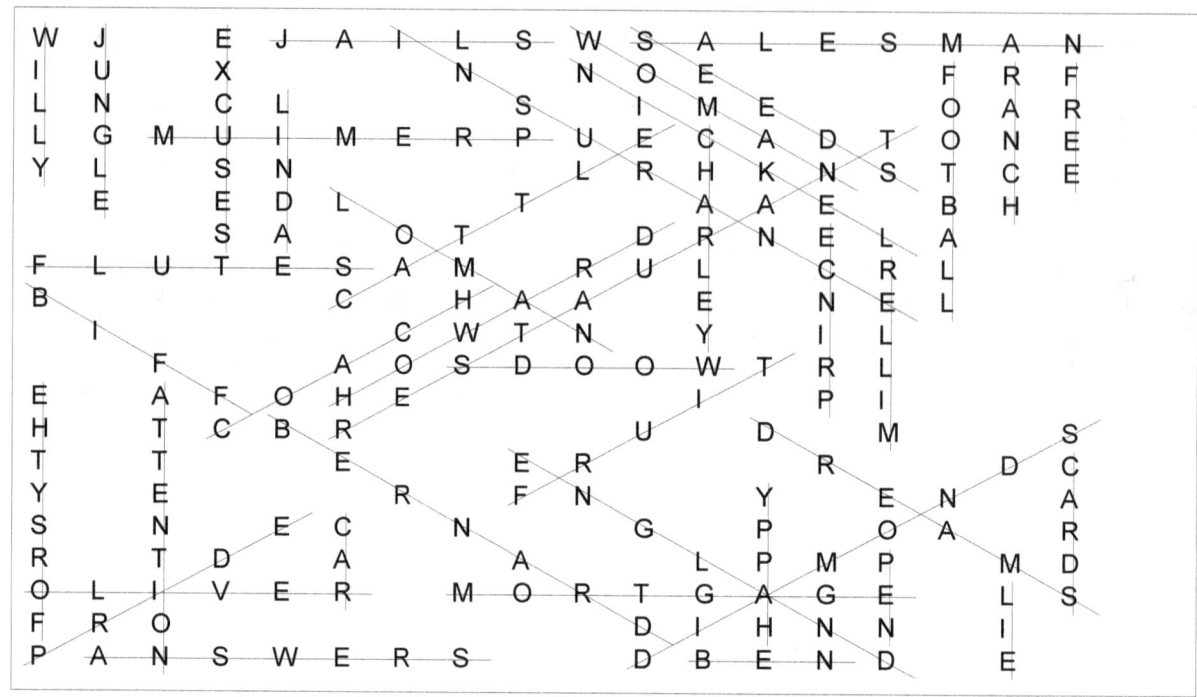

A man isn't a piece of ____ (5)
Author (6)
Ben walked into one and came out rich (6)
Biff calls Willy a 'fine, troubled ____' (6)
Biff stole one from school (8)
Biff took Bill Oliver's (3)
Biff wants money from Bill Oliver for this (5)
Bill____; Biff wants money from him (6)
Charley's son (7)
Death of a ____ (8)
Game Charley and Willy played (5)
Happy tries to pick her up at the restaurant (8)
He fires Willy (6)
He had all the wrong ____. All, all wrong. (6)
He loans Willy money (7)
He would probably congratulate Biff for his industriousness (5)
I realized what a ridiculous ____ my whole life has been (3)
Insurance payment (7)
Monthly house payment (8)
Person with whom Willy has a brief affair in Boston (5)
Ranch animals (6)
The ____ are burning, boys. (5)

The boys left Willy there (10)
The jungle is dark but full off ____ (8)
The salesman (5)
This is no time for false ____, Willy (5)
Transportation that helped Willy in life and to death (3)
We're ____ and clear (4)
What Linda makes for Willy's actions (7)
When a deposit bottle is broken, you can't get your ____ back (6)
Willy is the New ____ Man; he can't work in NY (7)
Willy wanted Bernard to give the test ____ to Biff (7)
Willy wanted to plant them (5)
Willy wants to borrow money from Charley to pay for it (9)
Willy's brother (3)
Willy's father made and sold them (6)
Willy's last name (5)
Willy's oldest son (4)
Willy's wife (5)
Willy's youngest son (5)
____ are full of fearless characters (5)
____ must be paid to such a person (9)

Death of a Salesman Word Search 3

Words are placed backwards, forward, diagonally, up and down. Words listed below are included in the maze. Circle the hidden vocabulary words in the maze.

```
W P F E H O W A R D M C V L W J G P P
K O O S N N D B Y X N O N N L U J R H
N W O J E G V W K X O A N O D N W I Q
B F T D B E L K T K I C R I C G G N C
P J B E S J D A C W T H T S W L C C F
P S A C T R K S N L N K M S B E E E S
L H L N P K F B J D E W T I C M D J P
H D L A X M E G A G T R O M J A I P K
B P Z R X C F R U I T C S M A E R D V
P E H U X M R C S F A K B O A E P D L
E N R S M S E T E L C O C C M N B C S
N B A N S W E R S U A R L I S A E A H
C I I I A I G X U T R Q U I J M N T S
F R C F L R C N C E C M K Y V S B T Y
Z A R K F L D H X S G S Y S B E V L G
P N Q S E H Q K E B M P L S H L R E A
P C M H M L P R S V P I L K X A G D J
E H T Y S R O F Y A A G I T S S N T S
D I A M O N D S H J C M W H X I B F P
C H A R L E Y L O M A N M I L L E R Y
```

| ANSWERS | DIAMONDS | INSURANCE | PREMIUM |
| ATTENTION | DREAMS | JAILS | PRIDE |
| BEN | ENGLAND | JUNGLE | PRINCE |
| BERNARD | EXCUSES | LIE | RANCH |
| BIFF | FLUTES | LINDA | SALESMAN |
| CAR | FOOTBALL | LOMAN | SEEDS |
| CARDS | FORSYTHE | MILLER | WILLY |
| CATTLE | FREE | MORTGAGE | WOMAN |
| CHARLEY | FRUIT | NICKEL | WOODS |
| COACH | HAPPY | OLIVER | |
| COMMISSION | HOWARD | PEN | |

Death of a Salesman Word Search 3 Answer Key

Words are placed backwards, forward, diagonally, up and down. Words listed below are included in the maze. Circle the hidden vocabulary words in the maze.

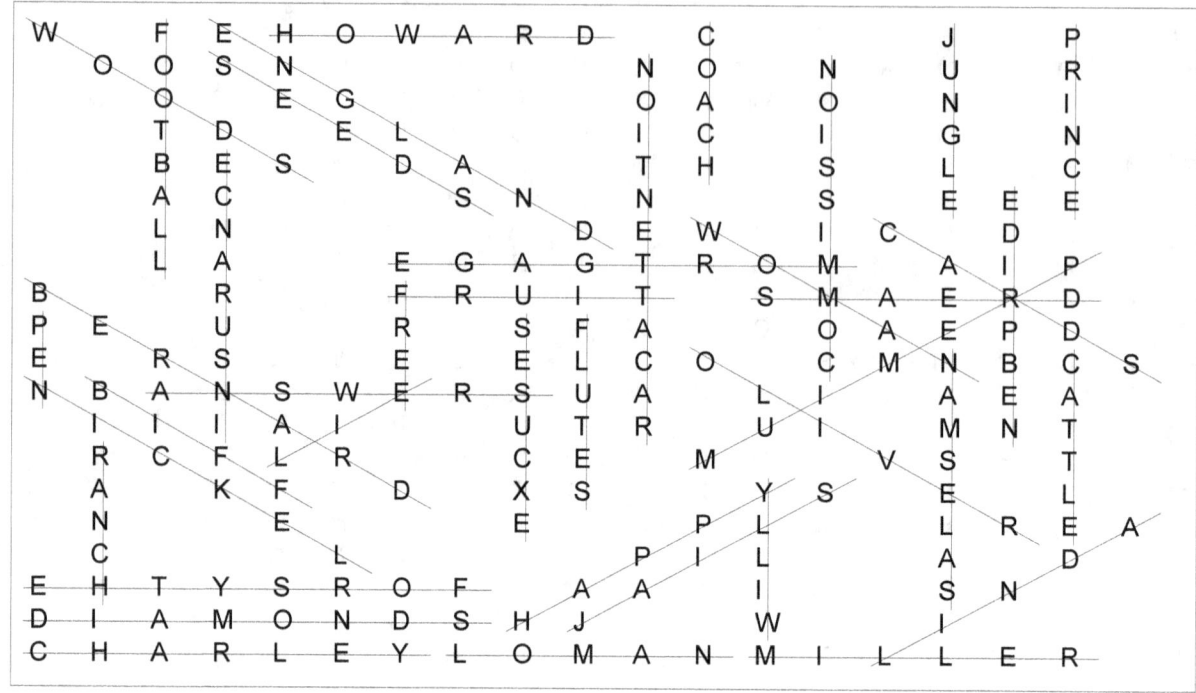

| ANSWERS | DIAMONDS | INSURANCE | PREMIUM |
| ATTENTION | DREAMS | JAILS | PRIDE |
| BEN | ENGLAND | JUNGLE | PRINCE |
| BERNARD | EXCUSES | LIE | RANCH |
| BIFF | FLUTES | LINDA | SALESMAN |
| CAR | FOOTBALL | LOMAN | SEEDS |
| CARDS | FORSYTHE | MILLER | WILLY |
| CATTLE | FREE | MORTGAGE | WOMAN |
| CHARLEY | FRUIT | NICKEL | WOODS |
| COACH | HAPPY | OLIVER | |
| COMMISSION | HOWARD | PEN | |

## Death of a Salesman Word Search 4

Words are placed backwards, forward, diagonally, up and down. Words listed below are included in the maze. Circle the hidden vocabulary words in the maze.

```
F O O T B A L L M O R T G A G E D N K
R C S M Z Z X Z D E L T T A C N O Z C
E V R E L L I M B Y I J D T A I D F Q
E P H F N R N K J N N M U L T J R L T
C O M M I S S I O N D L G N L L A F V
H B L Y W N U M D X A N E S G X N O L
Z T H L N D R F P L E T N Y A L R R F
C M C K I C A H R J T S J X N W E S P
C H N J C H N A E K E A S S O B Y M
Q C A J K S C P M R M E I L W O C T P
F S R R E M E P I W E D L L E D R H J
S W I L L Y J Y U J V S S P R S H E X
D C K Q C E F H M R E D T L S E M L X
R D B P J O Y L N S N C C A H D T A F
A Q C E E M A C U O C A D X U I P S N
W O M A N N E C M T L R B C A R D S Z
O M K A K I X A H W E I J W I P A B J
H G M B L E I V V A F S V N D X V N R
T O F W M D R R M F J V C E Z X Z B T
L F B H M Y M S W N C E Q F R U I T F
```

| ANSWERS | DIAMONDS | INSURANCE | PREMIUM |
| ATTENTION | DREAMS | JAILS | PRIDE |
| BEN | ENGLAND | JUNGLE | PRINCE |
| BERNARD | EXCUSES | LIE | RANCH |
| BIFF | FLUTES | LINDA | RESTAURANT |
| CAR | FOOTBALL | LOMAN | SALESMAN |
| CARDS | FORSYTHE | MILLER | SEEDS |
| CATTLE | FREE | MORTGAGE | WILLY |
| CHARLEY | FRUIT | NICKEL | WOMAN |
| COACH | HAPPY | OLIVER | WOODS |
| COMMISSION | HOWARD | PEN | |

Death of a Salesman Word Search 4 Answer Key

Words are placed backwards, forward, diagonally, up and down. Words listed below are included in the maze. Circle the hidden vocabulary words in the maze.

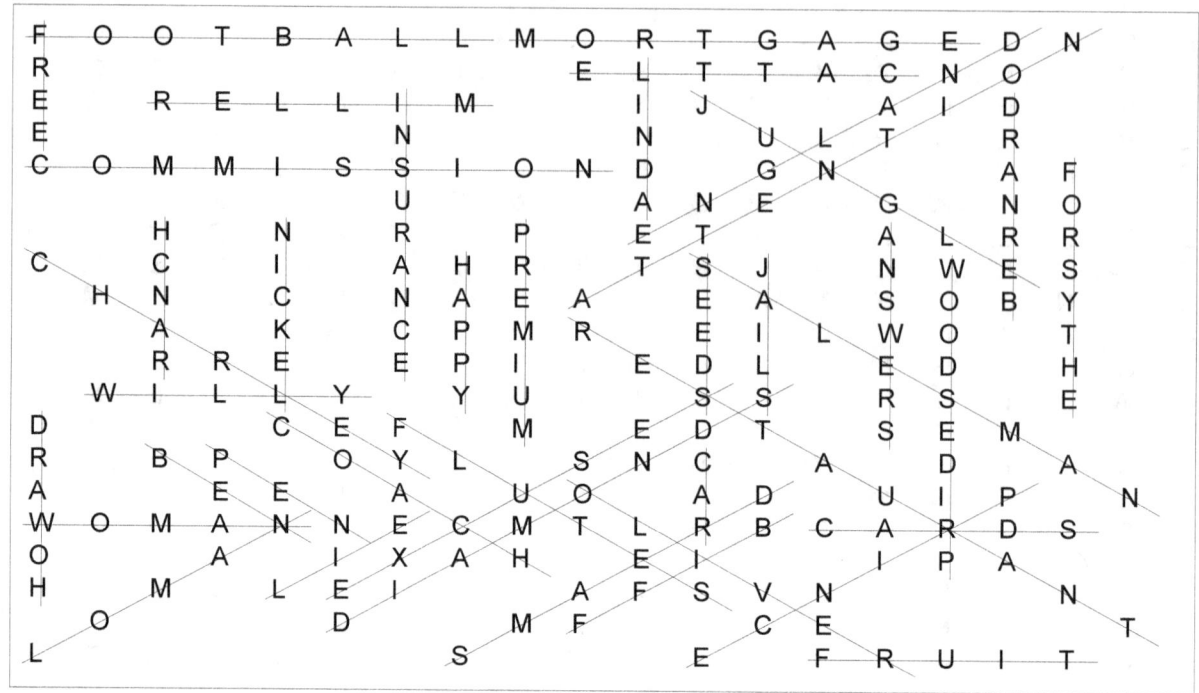

| ANSWERS | DIAMONDS | INSURANCE | PREMIUM |
| ATTENTION | DREAMS | JAILS | PRIDE |
| BEN | ENGLAND | JUNGLE | PRINCE |
| BERNARD | EXCUSES | LIE | RANCH |
| BIFF | FLUTES | LINDA | RESTAURANT |
| CAR | FOOTBALL | LOMAN | SALESMAN |
| CARDS | FORSYTHE | MILLER | SEEDS |
| CATTLE | FREE | MORTGAGE | WILLY |
| CHARLEY | FRUIT | NICKEL | WOMAN |
| COACH | HAPPY | OLIVER | WOODS |
| COMMISSION | HOWARD | PEN | |

Death of a Salesman Crossword 1

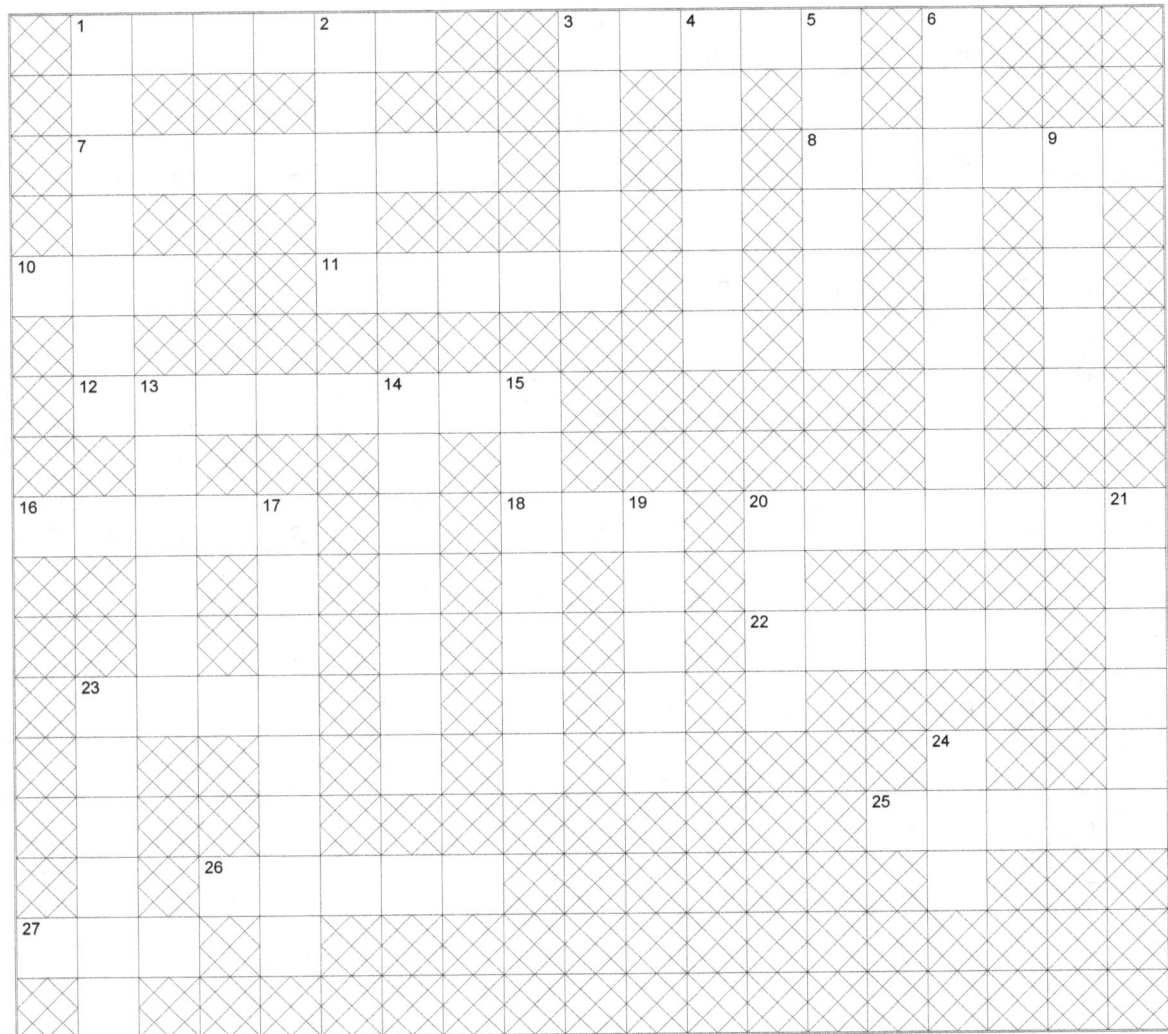

**Across**
1. Biff calls Willy a 'fine, troubled ____'
3. Person with whom Willy has a brief affair in Boston
7. Willy is the New ____ Man; he can't work in NY
8. Ranch animals
10. I realized what a ridiculous ____ my whole life has been
11. Willy's youngest son
12. Monthly house payment
16. ____ are full of fearless characters
18. Transportation that helped Willy in life and to death
20. Charley's son
22. A man isn't a piece of ____
23. We're ____ and clear
25. Willy wanted to plant them
26. Game Charley and Willy played
27. Willy's brother

**Down**
1. Insurance payment
2. He would probably congratulate Biff for his industriousness
3. The salesman
4. Author
5. When a deposit bottle is broken, you can't get your ____ back
6. ____ must be paid to such a person
9. Willy's last name
13. Bill____; Biff wants money from him
14. Willy wanted Bernard to give the test ____ to Biff
15. What Linda makes for Willy's actions
17. Death of a ____
19. Biff wants money from Bill Oliver for this
20. Willy's oldest son
21. He had all the wrong ____. All, all wrong.
23. Willy's father made and sold them
24. Biff took Bill Oliver's

# Death of a Salesman Crossword 1 Answer Key

|    | 1 P | R | I | N | 2 C | E |    | 3 W | 4 O | 5 M | A | 6 N |    | A |    |
|----|---|---|---|---|---|---|---|---|---|---|---|---|---|---|---|
|    | R |   |   |   | O |   |   | I |   | I |   | I |   | T |   |
|    | 7 E | N | G | L | A | N | D | L |   | L |   | 8 C | A | T | 9 L | E |
|    | M |   |   |   | C |   |   | L |   | L |   | K |   | E |   | O |
| 10 L | I | E |   |   | 11 H | A | P | P | Y |   | E |   | E |   | N |   | M |
|    | U |   |   |   |   |   |   |   |   |   | R |   | L |   | T |   | A |
|    | 12 M | 13 O | R | T | 14 G | A | 15 G | E |   |   |   |   | I |   | N |
|    |   | L |   |   | A |   | E | X |   |   |   |   | O |   |   |
| 16 J | A | 17 I | L | S |   | 18 S | C | A | 19 R |   | 20 B | E | R | N | A | R | 21 D |
|    |   | V |   |   | A |   |   | U |   | A |   | I |   |   |   |   | R |
|    |   | E |   |   | L |   |   | E |   | N |   | 22 F | R | U | I | T |   | E |
|    | 23 F | R | E | E |   | R |   | E |   | C |   | F |   |   |   |   | A |
|    | L |   |   |   | S |   |   | S |   | H |   |   |   | 24 P |   | M |
|    | U |   |   |   | M |   |   |   |   |   |   | 25 S | E | E | D | S |
|    | T |   | 26 C | A | R | D | S |   |   |   |   |   | N |   |   |
| 27 B | E | N |   | N |   |   |   |   |   |   |   |   |   |   |   |
|    | S |   |   |   |   |   |   |   |   |   |   |   |   |   |   |

## Across
1. Biff calls Willy a 'fine, troubled ____'
3. Person with whom Willy has a brief affair in Boston
7. Willy is the New ____ Man; he can't work in NY
8. Ranch animals
10. I realized what a ridiculous ____ my whole life has been
11. Willy's youngest son
12. Monthly house payment
16. ____ are full of fearless characters
18. Transportation that helped Willy in life and to death
20. Charley's son
22. A man isn't a piece of ____
23. We're ____ and clear
25. Willy wanted to plant them
26. Game Charley and Willy played
27. Willy's brother

## Down
1. Insurance payment
2. He would probably congratulate Biff for his industriousness
3. The salesman
4. Author
5. When a deposit bottle is broken, you can't get your ____ back
6. ____ must be paid to such a person
9. Willy's last name
13. Bill____; Biff wants money from him
14. Willy wanted Bernard to give the test ____ to Biff
15. What Linda makes for Willy's actions
17. Death of a ____
19. Biff wants money from Bill Oliver for this
20. Willy's oldest son
21. He had all the wrong ____. All, all wrong.
23. Willy's father made and sold them
24. Biff took Bill Oliver's

# Death of a Salesman Crossword 2

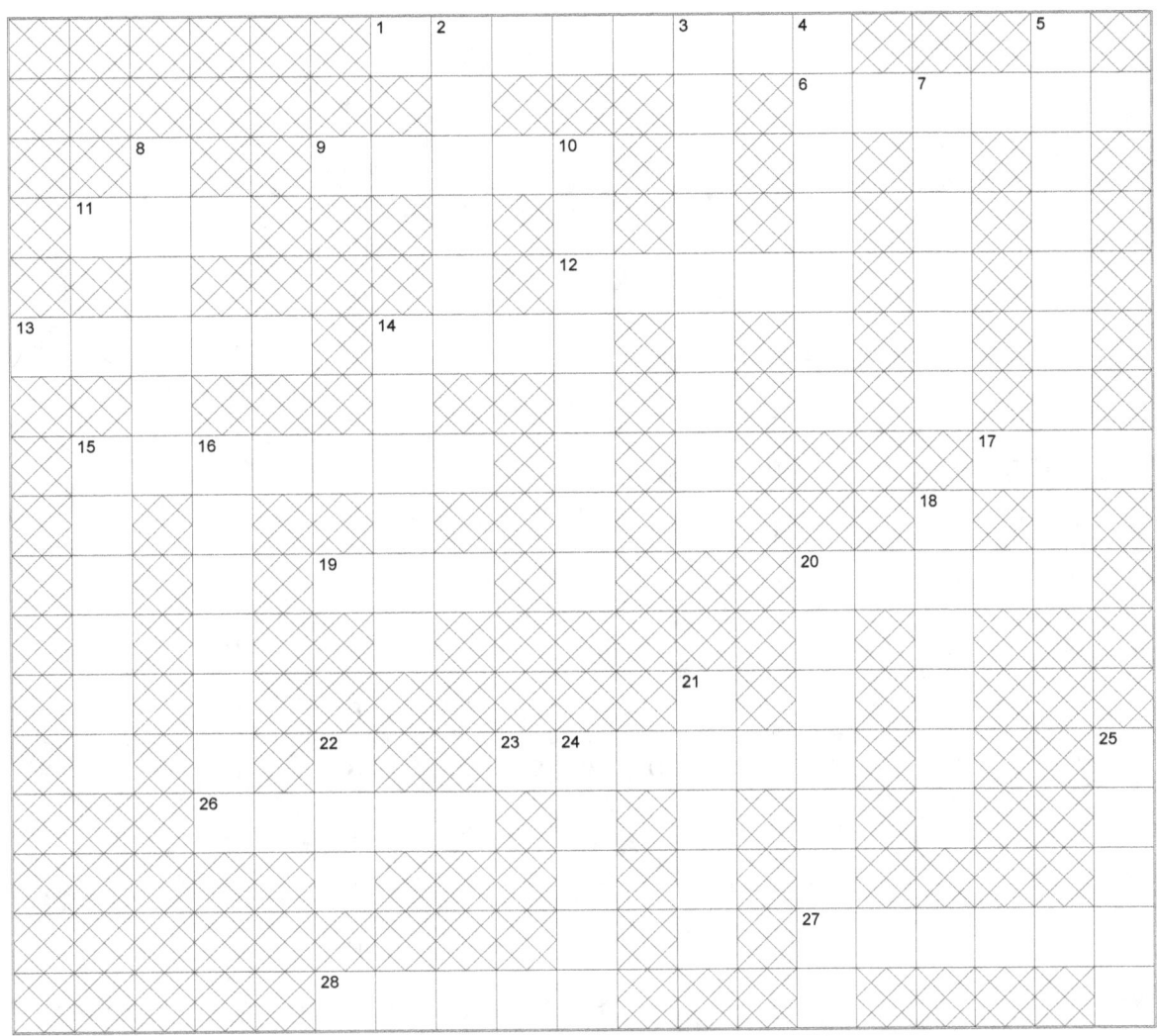

### Across
1. Monthly house payment
6. When a deposit bottle is broken, you can't get your ____ back
9. ____ are full of fearless characters
11. I realized what a ridiculous ____ my whole life has been
12. Willy's wife
13. The salesman
14. We're ____ and clear
15. Insurance payment
17. Transportation that helped Willy in life and to death
19. Biff took Bill Oliver's
20. A man isn't a piece of ____
23. He had all the wrong ____. All, all wrong.
26. Willy wanted to plant them
27. He fires Willy
28. He would probably congratulate Biff for his industriousness

### Down
2. Bill____; Biff wants money from him
3. ____ must be paid to such a person
4. Willy is the New ____ Man; he can't work in NY
5. The boys left Willy there
7. Ranch animals
8. Author
10. Death of a ____
14. Willy's father made and sold them
15. Biff calls Willy a 'fine, troubled ____'
16. What Linda makes for Willy's actions
18. Ben walked into one and came out rich
20. Happy tries to pick her up at the restaurant
21. Willy's youngest son
22. Willy's brother
24. Biff wants money from Bill Oliver for this
25. The ____ are burning, boys.

Death of a Salesman Crossword 2 Answer Key

|   |   |   |   |   | ¹M | ²O | R | T | ³G | A | G | ⁴E |   |   | ⁵R |   |
|---|---|---|---|---|---|---|---|---|---|---|---|---|---|---|---|---|
|   |   |   |   |   |   | L |   |   |   | T |   | ⁶N | I | ⁷C | K | E | L |
|   |   | ⁸M |   | ⁹J | A | I | ¹⁰L |   | T |   | G |   | A |   | S |   |
|   | ¹¹L | I | E |   |   | V |   | A |   | E |   | L |   | T |   | T |
|   |   | L |   |   |   | E |   | ¹²L | I | N | D | A |   | T |   | A |
| ¹³W | I | L | L | Y |   | ¹⁴F | R | E | E |   | T |   | N |   | L |   | U |
|   |   | E |   |   |   | L |   | S |   | I |   | D |   | E |   | R |
|   | ¹⁵P | R | ¹⁶E | M | I | U | M |   | M |   | O |   |   | ¹⁷C | A | R |
|   | R |   | X |   |   | T |   |   | A |   | N |   | ¹⁸J |   | N |
|   | I |   | C |   | ¹⁹P | E | N |   | N |   |   | ²⁰F | R | U | I | T |
|   | N |   | U |   |   | S |   |   |   |   |   | O |   | N |
|   | C |   | S |   |   |   |   |   | ²¹H |   |   | R |   | G |
|   | E |   | E |   | ²²B |   | ²³D | ²⁴R | E | A | M | S |   | L |   | ²⁵W |
|   |   |   | ²⁶S | E | E | D | S |   | A |   | P |   | Y |   | E |   | O |
|   |   |   |   |   | N |   |   | A |   | P |   | T |   | O |
|   |   |   |   |   |   |   |   | C |   | Y |   | ²⁷H | O | W | A | R | D |
|   |   |   |   | ²⁸C | O | A | C | H |   |   | E |   |   | S |

Across
1. Monthly house payment
6. When a deposit bottle is broken, you can't get your ____ back
9. ____ are full of fearless characters
11. I realized what a ridiculous ____ my whole life has been
12. Willy's wife
13. The salesman
14. We're ____ and clear
15. Insurance payment
17. Transportation that helped Willy in life and to death
19. Biff took Bill Oliver's
20. A man isn't a piece of ____
23. He had all the wrong ____. All, all wrong.
26. Willy wanted to plant them
27. He fires Willy
28. He would probably congratulate Biff for his industriousness

Down
2. Bill____; Biff wants money from him
3. ____ must be paid to such a person
4. Willy is the New ____ Man; he can't work in NY
5. The boys left Willy there
7. Ranch animals
8. Author
10. Death of a ____
14. Willy's father made and sold them
15. Biff calls Willy a 'fine, troubled ____'
16. What Linda makes for Willy's actions
18. Ben walked into one and came out rich
20. Happy tries to pick her up at the restaurant
21. Willy's youngest son
22. Willy's brother
24. Biff wants money from Bill Oliver for this
25. The ____ are burning, boys.

Death of a Salesman Crossword 3

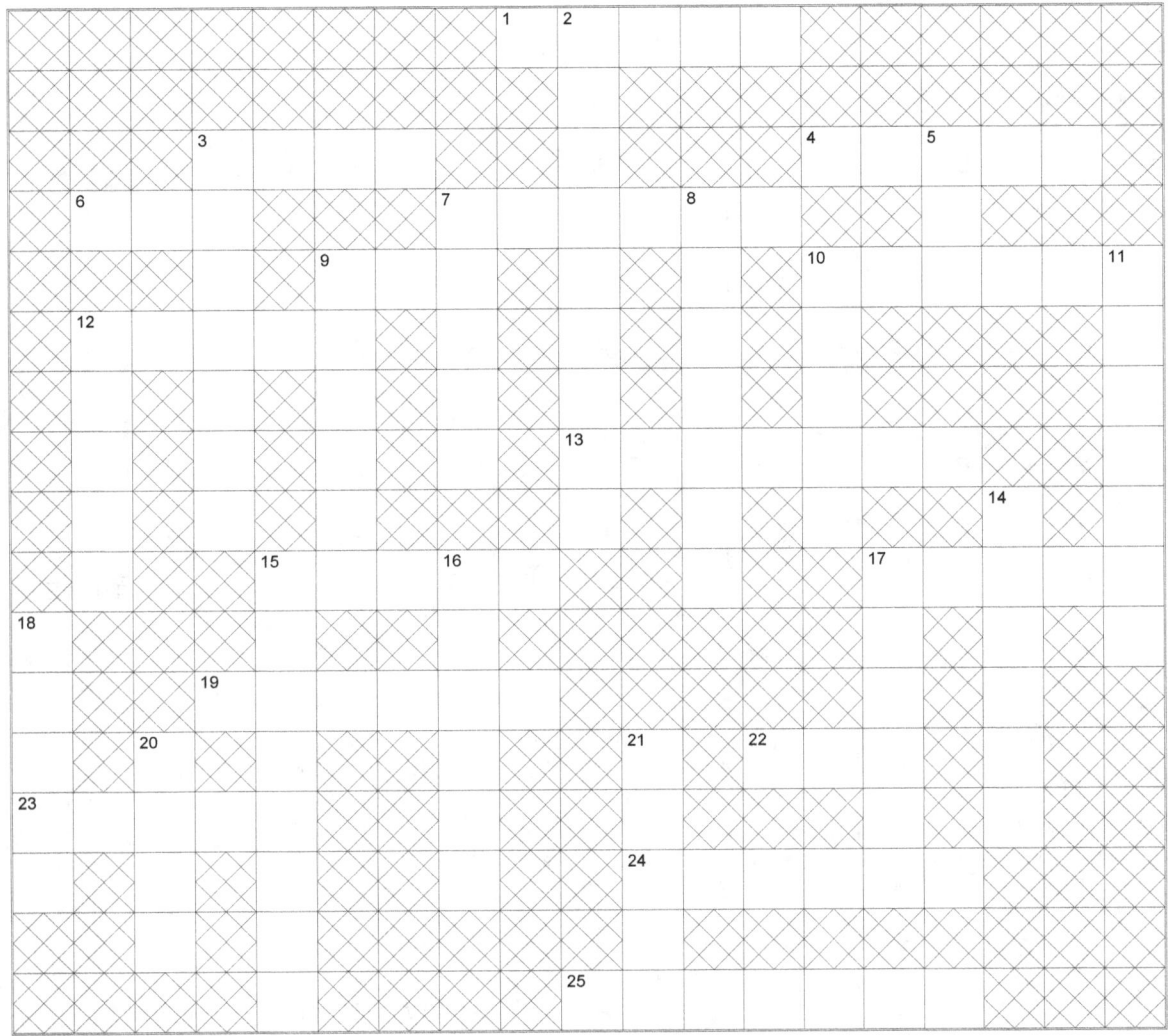

**Across**
1. The salesman
3. Willy's oldest son
4. Willy's youngest son
6. I realized what a ridiculous ____ my whole life has been
7. Willy's father made and sold them
9. Transportation that helped Willy in life and to death
10. Ben walked into one and came out rich
12. Willy's wife
13. He loans Willy money
15. Willy wanted to plant them
17. This is no time for false ____, Willy
19. Bill____; Biff wants money from him
22. Willy's brother
23. Game Charley and Willy played
24. Author
25. Willy wanted Bernard to give the test ____ to Biff

**Down**
2. Willy wants to borrow money from Charley to pay for it
3. Charley's son
5. Biff took Bill Oliver's
7. A man isn't a piece of ____
8. Willy is the New ____ Man; he can't work in NY
9. Ranch animals
10. ____ are full of fearless characters
11. What Linda makes for Willy's actions
12. Willy's last name
14. When a deposit bottle is broken, you can't get your ____ back
15. Death of a ____
16. He had all the wrong ____. All, all wrong.
17. Biff calls Willy a 'fine, troubled ____'
18. Biff wants money from Bill Oliver for this
20. We're ____ and clear
21. Person with whom Willy has a brief affair in Boston

Death of a Salesman Crossword 3 Answer Key

(Crossword grid with the following answers filled in)

Across:
1. WILLY
3. BIFF
4. HAPPY
6. LIE
7. FLUTES
9. CAR
10. JUNGLE
12. LINDA
13. CHARLEY
15. SEEDS
17. PRIDE
19. OLIVER
22. BEN
23. CARDS
24. MILLER
25. ANSWERS

Down:
2. INSURANCE
3. BERNARD
5. PEN
7. FRUIT
8. ENGLAND
9. CATTLE
10. JUNGLES
11. EXCUSE
12. LOMAN
14. NICKELS
15. SALESMAN
16. DREAMS
17. PRINCE
18. RACHEL
20. FREE
21. WOMAN

**Across**

1. The salesman
3. Willy's oldest son
4. Willy's youngest son
6. I realized what a ridiculous ____ my whole life has been
7. Willy's father made and sold them
9. Transportation that helped Willy in life and to death
10. Ben walked into one and came out rich
12. Willy's wife
13. He loans Willy money
15. Willy wanted to plant them
17. This is no time for false ____, Willy
19. Bill____; Biff wants money from him
22. Willy's brother
23. Game Charley and Willy played
24. Author
25. Willy wanted Bernard to give the test ____ to Biff

**Down**

2. Willy wants to borrow money from Charley to pay for it
3. Charley's son
5. Biff took Bill Oliver's
7. A man isn't a piece of ____
8. Willy is the New ____ Man; he can't work in NY
9. Ranch animals
10. ____ are full of fearless characters
11. What Linda makes for Willy's actions
12. Willy's last name
14. When a deposit bottle is broken, you can't get your ____ back
15. Death of a ____
16. He had all the wrong ____. All, all wrong.
17. Biff calls Willy a 'fine, troubled ____'
18. Biff wants money from Bill Oliver for this
20. We're ____ and clear
21. Person with whom Willy has a brief affair in Boston

Death of a Salesman Crossword 4

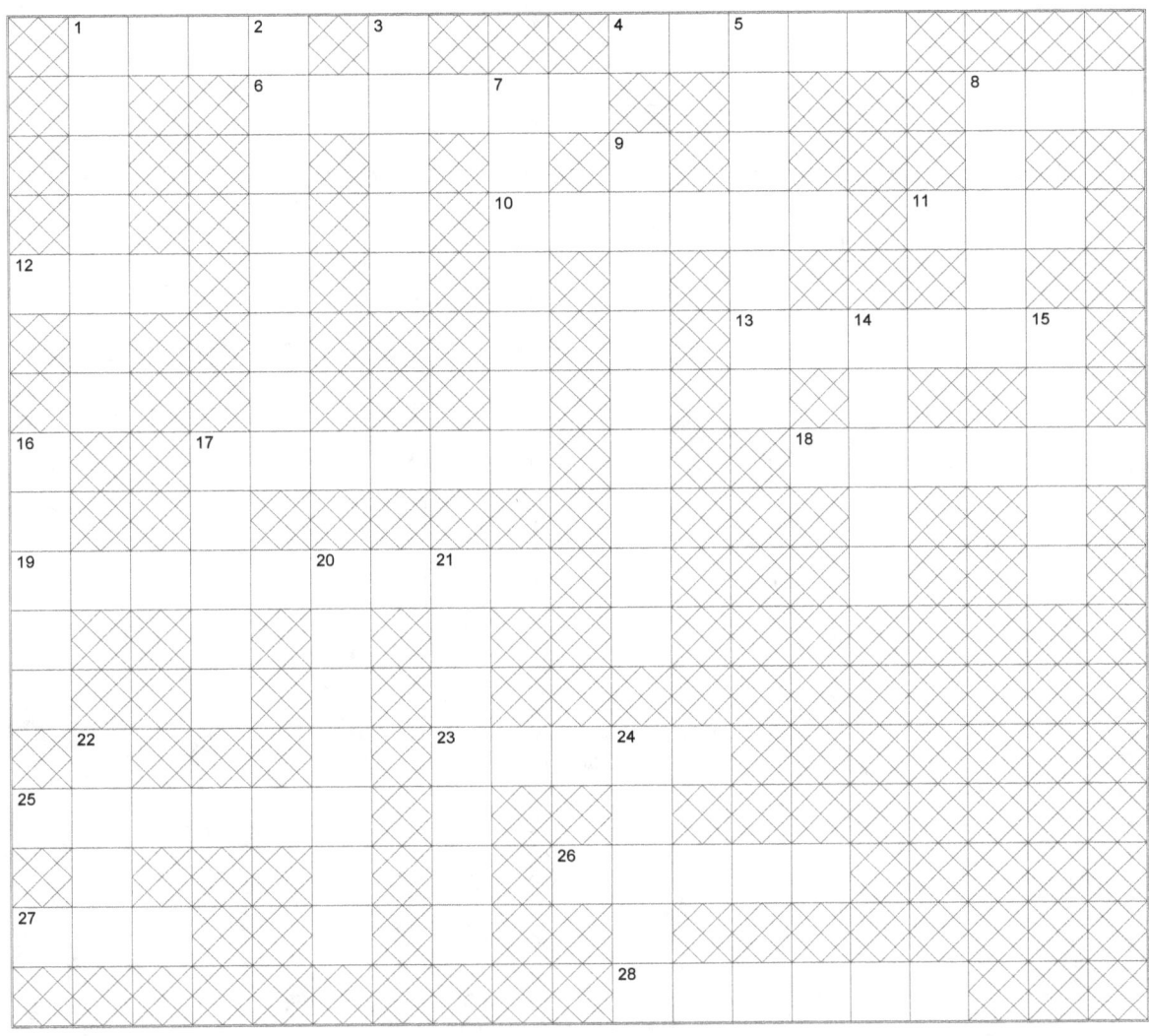

Across
1. Willy's oldest son
4. Willy wanted to plant them
6. Bill____; Biff wants money from him
8. Biff took Bill Oliver's
10. Ranch animals
11. I realized what a ridiculous ____ my whole life has been
12. Transportation that helped Willy in life and to death
13. When a deposit bottle is broken, you can't get your ____ back
17. Willy's father made and sold them
18. He had all the wrong ____. All, all wrong.
19. Willy wants to borrow money from Charley to pay for it
23. Biff wants money from Bill Oliver for this
25. Biff calls Willy a 'fine, troubled ____'
26. Willy's youngest son
27. Willy's brother
28. He fires Willy

Down
1. Charley's son
2. Biff stole one from school
3. The salesman
5. Willy is the New ____ Man; he can't work in NY
7. What Linda makes for Willy's actions
8. This is no time for false ____, Willy
9. ____ must be paid to such a person
14. Game Charley and Willy played
15. Willy's last name
16. ____ are full of fearless characters
17. A man isn't a piece of ____
20. Willy wanted Bernard to give the test ____ to Biff
21. He loans Willy money
22. We're ____ and clear
24. He would probably congratulate Biff for his industriousness

Death of a Salesman Crossword 4 Answer Key

|   | 1 B | I | 2 F | F |   | 3 W |   |   | 4 S | 5 E | E | D | S |   |   |   |
|---|---|---|---|---|---|---|---|---|---|---|---|---|---|---|---|---|
|   | E |   | 6 O | L | I | V | 7 E | R |   | N |   |   |   |   | 8 P | E | N |
|   | R |   | O |   | L |   | X |   | 9 A |   | G |   |   |   | R |   |
|   | N |   | T |   | L |   | 10 C | A | T | T | L | E |   | 11 L | I | E |
| 12 C | A | R | B |   | Y |   | U |   | T |   | A |   |   | D |   |
|   | R |   | A |   |   |   | S |   | E |   | 13 N | I | 14 C | K | E | 15 L |
|   | D |   | L |   |   |   | E |   | N |   | D |   | A |   |   | O |
| 16 J |   | 17 F | L | U | T | E | S |   | T |   | 18 D | R | E | A | M | S |
| A |   | R |   |   |   |   |   |   | I |   |   |   | D |   |   | A |
| 19 I | N | S | U | 20 R | A | 21 N | C | E |   | O |   |   |   | S |   | N |
| L |   | I |   | N |   | H |   |   |   | N |   |   |   |   |   |
| S |   | T |   | S |   | A |   |   |   |   |   |   |   |   |   |
|   | 22 F |   |   |   |   | 23 W | R | A | N | 24 C | H |   |   |   |   |
| 25 P | R | I | N | C | E |   | L |   |   | O |   |   |   |   |   |
|   | E |   |   |   |   |   | E |   | 26 H | A | P | P | Y |   |   |
| 27 B | E | N |   |   |   |   | S |   |   | C |   |   |   |   |   |
|   |   |   |   |   |   |   |   |   | 28 H | O | W | A | R | D |   |

**Across**
1. Willy's oldest son
4. Willy wanted to plant them
6. Bill____; Biff wants money from him
8. Biff took Bill Oliver's
10. Ranch animals
11. I realized what a ridiculous ____ my whole life has been
12. Transportation that helped Willy in life and to death
13. When a deposit bottle is broken, you can't get your ____ back
17. Willy's father made and sold them
18. He had all the wrong ____. All, all wrong.
19. Willy wants to borrow money from Charley to pay for it
23. Biff wants money from Bill Oliver for this
25. Biff calls Willy a 'fine, troubled ____'
26. Willy's youngest son
27. Willy's brother
28. He fires Willy

**Down**
1. Charley's son
2. Biff stole one from school
3. The salesman
5. Willy is the New ____ Man; he can't work in NY
7. What Linda makes for Willy's actions
8. This is no time for false ____, Willy
9. ____ must be paid to such a person
14. Game Charley and Willy played
15. Willy's last name
16. ____ are full of fearless characters
17. A man isn't a piece of ____
20. Willy wanted Bernard to give the test ____ to Biff
21. He loans Willy money
22. We're ____ and clear
24. He would probably congratulate Biff for his industriousness

44
Copyrighted

## Death of a Salesman

| | | | | |
|---|---|---|---|---|
| CARDS | FLUTES | COACH | PRINCE | CATTLE |
| BEN | HOWARD | INSURANCE | SALESMAN | CAR |
| BERNARD | JAILS | FREE SPACE | JUNGLE | WILLY |
| MILLER | DREAMS | ENGLAND | HAPPY | FREE |
| WOMAN | PEN | PRIDE | DIAMONDS | MORTGAGE |

## Death of a Salesman

| | | | | |
|---|---|---|---|---|
| FOOTBALL | OLIVER | CHARLEY | ANSWERS | SEEDS |
| LOMAN | LINDA | PREMIUM | WOODS | NICKEL |
| ATTENTION | BIFF | FREE SPACE | EXCUSES | FORSYTHE |
| RANCH | LIE | COMMISSION | MORTGAGE | DIAMONDS |
| PRIDE | PEN | WOMAN | FREE | HAPPY |

Death of a Salesman

| FREE | PREMIUM | FRUIT | LIE | ANSWERS |
|---|---|---|---|---|
| COMMISSION | EXCUSES | MILLER | RESTAURANT | SALESMAN |
| INSURANCE | ENGLAND | FREE SPACE | MORTGAGE | BIFF |
| CATTLE | WOODS | PEN | FORSYTHE | FLUTES |
| ATTENTION | FOOTBALL | JUNGLE | WOMAN | DREAMS |

Death of a Salesman

| BERNARD | HOWARD | NICKEL | DIAMONDS | PRIDE |
|---|---|---|---|---|
| CAR | JAILS | RANCH | SEEDS | HAPPY |
| PRINCE | OLIVER | FREE SPACE | COACH | LINDA |
| LOMAN | BEN | WILLY | DREAMS | WOMAN |
| JUNGLE | FOOTBALL | ATTENTION | FLUTES | FORSYTHE |

## Death of a Salesman

| PRIDE | FREE | LINDA | FOOTBALL | FRUIT |
|---|---|---|---|---|
| FLUTES | COMMISSION | DREAMS | JUNGLE | RANCH |
| MORTGAGE | OLIVER | FREE SPACE | LOMAN | HOWARD |
| BIFF | MILLER | SALESMAN | JAILS | RESTAURANT |
| ANSWERS | PRINCE | WOMAN | INSURANCE | EXCUSES |

## Death of a Salesman

| WILLY | PREMIUM | FORSYTHE | ATTENTION | WOODS |
|---|---|---|---|---|
| BEN | CATTLE | DIAMONDS | LIE | CARDS |
| SEEDS | NICKEL | FREE SPACE | CAR | ENGLAND |
| COACH | PEN | HAPPY | EXCUSES | INSURANCE |
| WOMAN | PRINCE | ANSWERS | RESTAURANT | JAILS |

Death of a Salesman

| OLIVER | BIFF | LOMAN | COACH | WOMAN |
|---|---|---|---|---|
| PRIDE | ANSWERS | CARDS | CATTLE | WILLY |
| JUNGLE | CAR | FREE SPACE | BERNARD | PRINCE |
| ENGLAND | LINDA | FLUTES | FRUIT | INSURANCE |
| CHARLEY | MORTGAGE | MILLER | BEN | SALESMAN |

Death of a Salesman

| ATTENTION | COMMISSION | FORSYTHE | NICKEL | RANCH |
|---|---|---|---|---|
| EXCUSES | PEN | JAILS | DREAMS | PREMIUM |
| WOODS | FOOTBALL | FREE SPACE | HOWARD | HAPPY |
| DIAMONDS | FREE | SEEDS | SALESMAN | BEN |
| MILLER | MORTGAGE | CHARLEY | INSURANCE | FRUIT |

Death of a Salesman

| CATTLE | CHARLEY | SALESMAN | DIAMONDS | HOWARD |
|---|---|---|---|---|
| WOMAN | ENGLAND | FOOTBALL | HAPPY | FLUTES |
| ATTENTION | OLIVER | FREE SPACE | PREMIUM | WOODS |
| PRIDE | PRINCE | RANCH | CAR | INSURANCE |
| ANSWERS | COACH | BEN | JAILS | MILLER |

Death of a Salesman

| JUNGLE | CARDS | LOMAN | COMMISSION | FRUIT |
|---|---|---|---|---|
| BERNARD | FREE | RESTAURANT | SEEDS | LINDA |
| LIE | NICKEL | FREE SPACE | FORSYTHE | DREAMS |
| MORTGAGE | EXCUSES | PEN | MILLER | JAILS |
| BEN | COACH | ANSWERS | INSURANCE | CAR |

49
Copyrighted

Death of a Salesman

| MILLER | INSURANCE | JAILS | PEN | NICKEL |
|---|---|---|---|---|
| BERNARD | LIE | FLUTES | RANCH | FOOTBALL |
| DIAMONDS | ANSWERS | FREE SPACE | COACH | FREE |
| ATTENTION | JUNGLE | CATTLE | ENGLAND | PRIDE |
| BEN | PREMIUM | CAR | FRUIT | HAPPY |

Death of a Salesman

| FORSYTHE | COMMISSION | SEEDS | HOWARD | LINDA |
|---|---|---|---|---|
| WOMAN | WILLY | PRINCE | LOMAN | MORTGAGE |
| CARDS | BIFF | FREE SPACE | CHARLEY | EXCUSES |
| RESTAURANT | SALESMAN | DREAMS | HAPPY | FRUIT |
| CAR | PREMIUM | BEN | PRIDE | ENGLAND |

Death of a Salesman

| BIFF | INSURANCE | FRUIT | ANSWERS | PRIDE |
|---|---|---|---|---|
| PREMIUM | HAPPY | CAR | WOMAN | COMMISSION |
| LOMAN | WILLY | FREE SPACE | ENGLAND | PRINCE |
| MILLER | RANCH | FOOTBALL | PEN | SEEDS |
| COACH | FORSYTHE | LIE | ATTENTION | JUNGLE |

Death of a Salesman

| CATTLE | BEN | MORTGAGE | DREAMS | HOWARD |
|---|---|---|---|---|
| CHARLEY | EXCUSES | CARDS | NICKEL | LINDA |
| DIAMONDS | BERNARD | FREE SPACE | FREE | WOODS |
| FLUTES | OLIVER | SALESMAN | JUNGLE | ATTENTION |
| LIE | FORSYTHE | COACH | SEEDS | PEN |

Death of a Salesman

| FORSYTHE | DREAMS | WILLY | MILLER | DIAMONDS |
|---|---|---|---|---|
| WOODS | OLIVER | JUNGLE | COMMISSION | PRINCE |
| FREE | MORTGAGE | FREE SPACE | PEN | BIFF |
| WOMAN | BERNARD | NICKEL | FLUTES | EXCUSES |
| FOOTBALL | PREMIUM | CARDS | LINDA | RANCH |

Death of a Salesman

| ATTENTION | FRUIT | JAILS | SEEDS | CATTLE |
|---|---|---|---|---|
| BEN | LOMAN | RESTAURANT | HOWARD | LIE |
| ENGLAND | COACH | FREE SPACE | SALESMAN | HAPPY |
| CAR | INSURANCE | CHARLEY | RANCH | LINDA |
| CARDS | PREMIUM | FOOTBALL | EXCUSES | FLUTES |

Death of a Salesman

| BIFF | PRIDE | FLUTES | CHARLEY | WOMAN |
|---|---|---|---|---|
| HAPPY | PREMIUM | PRINCE | PEN | HOWARD |
| WOODS | SEEDS | FREE SPACE | WILLY | LIE |
| RANCH | JUNGLE | ENGLAND | FOOTBALL | NICKEL |
| LINDA | CARDS | FORSYTHE | FREE | CAR |

Death of a Salesman

| SALESMAN | BERNARD | MILLER | FRUIT | BEN |
|---|---|---|---|---|
| ATTENTION | INSURANCE | CATTLE | JAILS | DIAMONDS |
| COMMISSION | COACH | FREE SPACE | LOMAN | ANSWERS |
| EXCUSES | OLIVER | DREAMS | CAR | FREE |
| FORSYTHE | CARDS | LINDA | NICKEL | FOOTBALL |

Death of a Salesman

| ENGLAND | NICKEL | HAPPY | FORSYTHE | JAILS |
|---|---|---|---|---|
| PRIDE | COACH | WOMAN | DREAMS | FOOTBALL |
| RESTAURANT | PRINCE | FREE SPACE | CAR | JUNGLE |
| BERNARD | WOODS | PREMIUM | CHARLEY | PEN |
| WILLY | MORTGAGE | INSURANCE | LINDA | HOWARD |

Death of a Salesman

| LOMAN | SALESMAN | RANCH | BIFF | OLIVER |
|---|---|---|---|---|
| EXCUSES | DIAMONDS | SEEDS | FREE | LIE |
| BEN | COMMISSION | FREE SPACE | FLUTES | CARDS |
| ANSWERS | ATTENTION | FRUIT | HOWARD | LINDA |
| INSURANCE | MORTGAGE | WILLY | PEN | CHARLEY |

## Death of a Salesman

| ENGLAND | CAR | CHARLEY | BERNARD | BIFF |
|---|---|---|---|---|
| COMMISSION | WILLY | INSURANCE | LIE | ATTENTION |
| JAILS | JUNGLE | FREE SPACE | RESTAURANT | FREE |
| FOOTBALL | WOODS | MORTGAGE | RANCH | FLUTES |
| CATTLE | CARDS | COACH | ANSWERS | NICKEL |

## Death of a Salesman

| LOMAN | FRUIT | EXCUSES | LINDA | DREAMS |
|---|---|---|---|---|
| BEN | HAPPY | DIAMONDS | WOMAN | PRIDE |
| FORSYTHE | OLIVER | FREE SPACE | SALESMAN | SEEDS |
| PRINCE | PREMIUM | MILLER | NICKEL | ANSWERS |
| COACH | CARDS | CATTLE | FLUTES | RANCH |

Death of a Salesman

| RESTAURANT | ENGLAND | LOMAN | FREE | LINDA |
|---|---|---|---|---|
| DIAMONDS | PREMIUM | HOWARD | HAPPY | CARDS |
| DREAMS | COMMISSION | FREE SPACE | JUNGLE | MORTGAGE |
| FRUIT | RANCH | EXCUSES | NICKEL | PEN |
| PRIDE | CHARLEY | FOOTBALL | ANSWERS | BERNARD |

Death of a Salesman

| FLUTES | WOODS | MILLER | LIE | WILLY |
|---|---|---|---|---|
| OLIVER | INSURANCE | BIFF | FORSYTHE | CAR |
| ATTENTION | COACH | FREE SPACE | SEEDS | SALESMAN |
| JAILS | WOMAN | CATTLE | BERNARD | ANSWERS |
| FOOTBALL | CHARLEY | PRIDE | PEN | NICKEL |

Death of a Salesman

| COACH | FORSYTHE | WILLY | ANSWERS | RANCH |
|---|---|---|---|---|
| NICKEL | SALESMAN | WOMAN | ATTENTION | LINDA |
| JAILS | CAR | FREE SPACE | BERNARD | INSURANCE |
| CARDS | FLUTES | DREAMS | BIFF | MILLER |
| OLIVER | FREE | EXCUSES | FOOTBALL | LIE |

Death of a Salesman

| SEEDS | MORTGAGE | PRIDE | WOODS | CHARLEY |
|---|---|---|---|---|
| COMMISSION | PRINCE | RESTAURANT | PREMIUM | CATTLE |
| BEN | LOMAN | FREE SPACE | HAPPY | PEN |
| JUNGLE | DIAMONDS | HOWARD | LIE | FOOTBALL |
| EXCUSES | FREE | OLIVER | MILLER | BIFF |

Death of a Salesman

| ATTENTION | EXCUSES | COACH | MILLER | FLUTES |
|---|---|---|---|---|
| WOODS | FOOTBALL | FORSYTHE | RANCH | CHARLEY |
| ANSWERS | WOMAN | FREE SPACE | PREMIUM | LOMAN |
| DIAMONDS | JUNGLE | MORTGAGE | DREAMS | FREE |
| WILLY | FRUIT | PRINCE | LINDA | BERNARD |

Death of a Salesman

| CAR | OLIVER | CARDS | INSURANCE | ENGLAND |
|---|---|---|---|---|
| HAPPY | PEN | CATTLE | HOWARD | SALESMAN |
| COMMISSION | PRIDE | FREE SPACE | LIE | BEN |
| BIFF | SEEDS | RESTAURANT | BERNARD | LINDA |
| PRINCE | FRUIT | WILLY | FREE | DREAMS |

Death of a Salesman

| CARDS | FLUTES | LOMAN | CAR | LINDA |
|---|---|---|---|---|
| JAILS | ANSWERS | DREAMS | BEN | EXCUSES |
| PREMIUM | MILLER | FREE SPACE | NICKEL | FRUIT |
| FREE | RESTAURANT | PRINCE | WILLY | PRIDE |
| JUNGLE | ENGLAND | COMMISSION | WOMAN | PEN |

Death of a Salesman

| DIAMONDS | FOOTBALL | WOODS | BERNARD | HOWARD |
|---|---|---|---|---|
| LIE | OLIVER | ATTENTION | MORTGAGE | COACH |
| SALESMAN | RANCH | FREE SPACE | SEEDS | INSURANCE |
| CATTLE | CHARLEY | FORSYTHE | PEN | WOMAN |
| COMMISSION | ENGLAND | JUNGLE | PRIDE | WILLY |

Death of a Salesman

| FRUIT | RANCH | SALESMAN | PEN | NICKEL |
|---|---|---|---|---|
| FLUTES | WOODS | OLIVER | ATTENTION | FORSYTHE |
| DREAMS | MILLER | FREE SPACE | ENGLAND | HOWARD |
| MORTGAGE | DIAMONDS | WILLY | LIE | CARDS |
| BERNARD | LINDA | LOMAN | JUNGLE | COMMISSION |

Death of a Salesman

| ANSWERS | PREMIUM | SEEDS | HAPPY | EXCUSES |
|---|---|---|---|---|
| BEN | BIFF | INSURANCE | CAR | COACH |
| CHARLEY | WOMAN | FREE SPACE | RESTAURANT | FOOTBALL |
| CATTLE | JAILS | PRIDE | COMMISSION | JUNGLE |
| LOMAN | LINDA | BERNARD | CARDS | LIE |

# Death of a Salesman Vocabulary Word List

| No. | Word | Clue/Definition |
|---|---|---|
| 1. | AGITATION | Disturbance; annoyance |
| 2. | AGONIZED | Suffering great anguish; struggling |
| 3. | ANXIOUSLY | With a worried eagerness |
| 4. | AVIDLY | Enthusiastically; with great interest |
| 5. | BEFUDDLED | Confused |
| 6. | CANDIDLY | Characterized by openness; frankly; straightforward |
| 7. | CLINCHES | Settles something conclusively |
| 8. | COMRADESHIP | Friendship; friendly spirit of working together |
| 9. | CONTEMPTUOUS | Dishonorable; disgraceful |
| 10. | DICTATION | To say aloud to be recorded & then written by another from the recording |
| 11. | DISPEL | To rid one's mind of |
| 12. | ENTHRALLED | Held spellbound; captivated |
| 13. | FALTERS | Stumbles; moves unsteadily |
| 14. | GIST | Main idea |
| 15. | IDEALIST | One who sees the best in things; a dreamer; not realistic |
| 16. | IMITATED | Copied mannerisms, actions or speech |
| 17. | IMPLACABLY | In a manner showing unwillingness to make peace |
| 18. | INCARNATE | Personified; given a human form |
| 19. | INCIPIENT | Beginning to exist |
| 20. | INCREDULOUSLY | Unbelievingly |
| 21. | INSINUATES | Becomes introduced gradually |
| 22. | INTENT | Concentrating; engrossed |
| 23. | LACONIC | Using few words |
| 24. | LIABLE | Likely; at risk of experiencing something unpleasant |
| 25. | MERCURIAL | Quick & changeable in temperament |
| 26. | OMINOUSLY | Threateningly |
| 27. | OVEREMPHASIZE | Place too much importance on |
| 28. | OVERSTRUNG | Pushed to one's emotional limits |
| 29. | PHILANDERING | Engaging in many casual love affairs |
| 30. | RAUCOUS | Rough-sounding; harsh; boisterous |
| 31. | REMISS | Not attending to duty; negligent; careless |
| 32. | SENSUOUS | Appealing to the senses |
| 33. | SENTIMENT | Tender, romantic or nostalgic feeling |
| 34. | SOLIDIFIED | Made strong, sturdy or stable |
| 35. | SOLITARY | Existing alone |
| 36. | STRIVING | Struggling; working |
| 37. | SUBDUED | Made less intense; toned down; softened |
| 38. | TREPIDATION | A state of alarm or dread |

Copyrighted

Death of a Salesman Vocabulary Fill In The Blanks 1

_____ 1. Dishonorable; disgraceful

_____ 2. Settles something conclusively

_____ 3. Suffering great anguish; struggling

_____ 4. Beginning to exist

_____ 5. Concentrating; engrossed

_____ 6. Confused

_____ 7. Characterized by openness; frankly; straightforward

_____ 8. To say aloud to be recorded & then written by another from the recording

_____ 9. Engaging in many casual love affairs

_____ 10. Personified; given a human form

_____ 11. Copied mannerisms, actions or speech

_____ 12. Threateningly

_____ 13. Existing alone

_____ 14. Likely; at risk of experiencing something unpleasant

_____ 15. In a manner showing unwillingness to make peace

_____ 16. A state of alarm or dread

_____ 17. Made less intense; toned down; softened

_____ 18. To rid one's mind of

_____ 19. Stumbles; moves unsteadily

_____ 20. Appealing to the senses

Death of a Salesman Vocabulary Fill In The Blanks 1 Answer Key

|  |  |
|---|---|
| CONTEMPTUOUS | 1. Dishonorable; disgraceful |
| CLINCHES | 2. Settles something conclusively |
| AGONIZED | 3. Suffering great anguish; struggling |
| INCIPIENT | 4. Beginning to exist |
| INTENT | 5. Concentrating; engrossed |
| BEFUDDLED | 6. Confused |
| CANDIDLY | 7. Characterized by openness; frankly; straightforward |
| DICTATION | 8. To say aloud to be recorded & then written by another from the recording |
| PHILANDERING | 9. Engaging in many casual love affairs |
| INCARNATE | 10. Personified; given a human form |
| IMITATED | 11. Copied mannerisms, actions or speech |
| OMINOUSLY | 12. Threateningly |
| SOLITARY | 13. Existing alone |
| LIABLE | 14. Likely; at risk of experiencing something unpleasant |
| IMPLACABLY | 15. In a manner showing unwillingness to make peace |
| TREPIDATION | 16. A state of alarm or dread |
| SUBDUED | 17. Made less intense; toned down; softened |
| DISPEL | 18. To rid one's mind of |
| FALTERS | 19. Stumbles; moves unsteadily |
| SENSUOUS | 20. Appealing to the senses |

Death of a Salesman Vocabulary Fill In The Blanks 2

_____  1. Using few words
_____  2. Not attending to duty; negligent; careless
_____  3. Beginning to exist
_____  4. Copied mannerisms, actions or speech
_____  5. A state of alarm or dread
_____  6. Characterized by openness; frankly; straightforward
_____  7. Appealing to the senses
_____  8. Rough-sounding; harsh; boisterous
_____  9. Personified; given a human form
_____ 10. Stumbles; moves unsteadily
_____ 11. Dishonorable; disgraceful
_____ 12. Main idea
_____ 13. Settles something conclusively
_____ 14. Confused
_____ 15. Concentrating; engrossed
_____ 16. Becomes introduced gradually
_____ 17. Friendship; friendly spirit of working together
_____ 18. To say aloud to be recorded & then written by another from the recording
_____ 19. Made less intense; toned down; softened
_____ 20. Disturbance; annoyance

Death of a Salesman Vocabulary Fill In The Blanks 2 Answer Key

|  |  |
|---|---|
| LACONIC | 1. Using few words |
| REMISS | 2. Not attending to duty; negligent; careless |
| INCIPIENT | 3. Beginning to exist |
| IMITATED | 4. Copied mannerisms, actions or speech |
| TREPIDATION | 5. A state of alarm or dread |
| CANDIDLY | 6. Characterized by openness; frankly; straightforward |
| SENSUOUS | 7. Appealing to the senses |
| RAUCOUS | 8. Rough-sounding; harsh; boisterous |
| INCARNATE | 9. Personified; given a human form |
| FALTERS | 10. Stumbles; moves unsteadily |
| CONTEMPTUOUS | 11. Dishonorable; disgraceful |
| GIST | 12. Main idea |
| CLINCHES | 13. Settles something conclusively |
| BEFUDDLED | 14. Confused |
| INTENT | 15. Concentrating; engrossed |
| INSINUATES | 16. Becomes introduced gradually |
| COMRADESHIP | 17. Friendship; friendly spirit of working together |
| DICTATION | 18. To say aloud to be recorded & then written by another from the recording |
| SUBDUED | 19. Made less intense; toned down; softened |
| AGITATION | 20. Disturbance; annoyance |

Death of a Salesman Vocabulary Fill In The Blanks 3

_____    1. Confused
_____    2. Personified; given a human form
_____    3. Tender, romantic or nostalgic feeling
_____    4. Place too much importance on
_____    5. Characterized by openness; frankly; straightforward
_____    6. To rid one's mind of
_____    7. A state of alarm or dread
_____    8. Unbelievingly
_____    9. Suffering great anguish; struggling
_____   10. Made less intense; toned down; softened
_____   11. Enthusiastically; with great interest
_____   12. Dishonorable; disgraceful
_____   13. Struggling; working
_____   14. Appealing to the senses
_____   15. Engaging in many casual love affairs
_____   16. Rough-sounding; harsh; boisterous
_____   17. Made strong, sturdy or stable
_____   18. Existing alone
_____   19. Using few words
_____   20. Copied mannerisms, actions or speech

Death of a Salesman Vocabulary Fill In The Blanks 3 Answer Key

|  |  |
|---|---|
| BEFUDDLED | 1. Confused |
| INCARNATE | 2. Personified; given a human form |
| SENTIMENT | 3. Tender, romantic or nostalgic feeling |
| OVEREMPHASIZE | 4. Place too much importance on |
| CANDIDLY | 5. Characterized by openness; frankly; straightforward |
| DISPEL | 6. To rid one's mind of |
| TREPIDATION | 7. A state of alarm or dread |
| INCREDULOUSLY | 8. Unbelievingly |
| AGONIZED | 9. Suffering great anguish; struggling |
| SUBDUED | 10. Made less intense; toned down; softened |
| AVIDLY | 11. Enthusiastically; with great interest |
| CONTEMPTUOUS | 12. Dishonorable; disgraceful |
| STRIVING | 13. Struggling; working |
| SENSUOUS | 14. Appealing to the senses |
| PHILANDERING | 15. Engaging in many casual love affairs |
| RAUCOUS | 16. Rough-sounding; harsh; boisterous |
| SOLIDIFIED | 17. Made strong, sturdy or stable |
| SOLITARY | 18. Existing alone |
| LACONIC | 19. Using few words |
| IMITATED | 20. Copied mannerisms, actions or speech |

Death of a Salesman Vocabulary Fill In The Blanks 4

_____  1. Struggling; working

_____  2. To say aloud to be recorded & then written by another from the recording

_____  3. Unbelievingly

_____  4. Threateningly

_____  5. Using few words

_____  6. A state of alarm or dread

_____  7. Main idea

_____  8. Place too much importance on

_____  9. Personified; given a human form

_____  10. Disturbance; annoyance

_____  11. Settles something conclusively

_____  12. Becomes introduced gradually

_____  13. Concentrating; engrossed

_____  14. Enthusiastically; with great interest

_____  15. Copied mannerisms, actions or speech

_____  16. To rid one's mind of

_____  17. Appealing to the senses

_____  18. Held spellbound; captivated

_____  19. Suffering great anguish; struggling

_____  20. Likely; at risk of experiencing something unpleasant

Death of a Salesman Vocabulary Fill In The Blanks 4 Answer Key

|  |  |
|---|---|
| STRIVING | 1. Struggling; working |
| DICTATION | 2. To say aloud to be recorded & then written by another from the recording |
| INCREDULOUSLY | 3. Unbelievingly |
| OMINOUSLY | 4. Threateningly |
| LACONIC | 5. Using few words |
| TREPIDATION | 6. A state of alarm or dread |
| GIST | 7. Main idea |
| OVEREMPHASIZE | 8. Place too much importance on |
| INCARNATE | 9. Personified; given a human form |
| AGITATION | 10. Disturbance; annoyance |
| CLINCHES | 11. Settles something conclusively |
| INSINUATES | 12. Becomes introduced gradually |
| INTENT | 13. Concentrating; engrossed |
| AVIDLY | 14. Enthusiastically; with great interest |
| IMITATED | 15. Copied mannerisms, actions or speech |
| DISPEL | 16. To rid one's mind of |
| SENSUOUS | 17. Appealing to the senses |
| ENTHRALLED | 18. Held spellbound; captivated |
| AGONIZED | 19. Suffering great anguish; struggling |
| LIABLE | 20. Likely; at risk of experiencing something unpleasant |

Death of a Salesman Vocabulary Matching 1

___ 1. GIST
___ 2. RAUCOUS
___ 3. INSINUATES
___ 4. SUBDUED
___ 5. IMPLACABLY
___ 6. TREPIDATION
___ 7. INCREDULOUSLY
___ 8. CANDIDLY
___ 9. ENTHRALLED
___ 10. OMINOUSLY
___ 11. REMISS
___ 12. INCARNATE
___ 13. BEFUDDLED
___ 14. IDEALIST
___ 15. CLINCHES
___ 16. OVEREMPHASIZE
___ 17. LIABLE
___ 18. MERCURIAL
___ 19. INCIPIENT
___ 20. SENTIMENT
___ 21. AVIDLY
___ 22. OVERSTRUNG
___ 23. CONTEMPTUOUS
___ 24. DICTATION
___ 25. COMRADESHIP

A. To say aloud to be recorded & then written by another from the recording
B. Tender, romantic or nostalgic feeling
C. Dishonorable; disgraceful
D. Enthusiastically; with great interest
E. Friendship; friendly spirit of working together
F. Threateningly
G. Unbelievingly
H. Settles something conclusively
I. Not attending to duty; negligent; careless
J. In a manner showing unwillingness to make peace
K. Likely; at risk of experiencing something unpleasant
L. Confused
M. Pushed to one's emotional limits
N. Held spellbound; captivated
O. Quick & changeable in temperament
P. Place too much importance on
Q. Personified; given a human form
R. Main idea
S. Made less intense; toned down; softened
T. Characterized by openness; frankly; straightforward
U. Becomes introduced gradually
V. One who sees the best in things; a dreamer; not realistic
W. Beginning to exist
X. Rough-sounding; harsh; boisterous
Y. A state of alarm or dread

Death of a Salesman Vocabulary Matching 1 Answer Key

| | |
|---|---|
| R - 1. GIST | A. To say aloud to be recorded & then written by another from the recording |
| X - 2. RAUCOUS | B. Tender, romantic or nostalgic feeling |
| U - 3. INSINUATES | C. Dishonorable; disgraceful |
| S - 4. SUBDUED | D. Enthusiastically; with great interest |
| J - 5. IMPLACABLY | E. Friendship; friendly spirit of working together |
| Y - 6. TREPIDATION | F. Threateningly |
| G - 7. INCREDULOUSLY | G. Unbelievingly |
| T - 8. CANDIDLY | H. Settles something conclusively |
| N - 9. ENTHRALLED | I. Not attending to duty; negligent; careless |
| F - 10. OMINOUSLY | J. In a manner showing unwillingness to make peace |
| I - 11. REMISS | K. Likely; at risk of experiencing something unpleasant |
| Q - 12. INCARNATE | L. Confused |
| L - 13. BEFUDDLED | M. Pushed to one's emotional limits |
| V - 14. IDEALIST | N. Held spellbound; captivated |
| H - 15. CLINCHES | O. Quick & changeable in temperament |
| P - 16. OVEREMPHASIZE | P. Place too much importance on |
| K - 17. LIABLE | Q. Personified; given a human form |
| O - 18. MERCURIAL | R. Main idea |
| W - 19. INCIPIENT | S. Made less intense; toned down; softened |
| B - 20. SENTIMENT | T. Characterized by openness; frankly; straightforward |
| D - 21. AVIDLY | U. Becomes introduced gradually |
| M - 22. OVERSTRUNG | V. One who sees the best in things; a dreamer; not realistic |
| C - 23. CONTEMPTUOUS | W. Beginning to exist |
| A - 24. DICTATION | X. Rough-sounding; harsh; boisterous |
| E - 25. COMRADESHIP | Y. A state of alarm or dread |

Death of a Salesman Vocabulary Matching 2

___ 1. SENSUOUS
___ 2. SOLIDIFIED
___ 3. BEFUDDLED
___ 4. OVERSTRUNG
___ 5. IMPLACABLY
___ 6. CANDIDLY
___ 7. CLINCHES
___ 8. INCIPIENT
___ 9. PHILANDERING
___10. LACONIC
___11. DICTATION
___12. OMINOUSLY
___13. OVEREMPHASIZE
___14. TREPIDATION
___15. SUBDUED
___16. ENTHRALLED
___17. AGONIZED
___18. DISPEL
___19. LIABLE
___20. INTENT
___21. RAUCOUS
___22. SOLITARY
___23. AVIDLY
___24. COMRADESHIP
___25. MERCURIAL

A. Pushed to one's emotional limits
B. Beginning to exist
C. A state of alarm or dread
D. Settles something conclusively
E. To rid one's mind of
F. Enthusiastically; with great interest
G. Likely; at risk of experiencing something unpleasant
H. Appealing to the senses
I. To say aloud to be recorded & then written by another from the recording
J. Threateningly
K. Made less intense; toned down; softened
L. Confused
M. Rough-sounding; harsh; boisterous
N. Suffering great anguish; struggling
O. Quick & changeable in temperament
P. Using few words
Q. Existing alone
R. Place too much importance on
S. Concentrating; engrossed
T. Held spellbound; captivated
U. Engaging in many casual love affairs
V. Characterized by openness; frankly; straightforward
W. Made strong, sturdy or stable
X. Friendship; friendly spirit of working together
Y. In a manner showing unwillingness to make peace

Death of a Salesman Vocabulary Matching 2 Answer Key

| | | |
|---|---|---|
| H - 1. SENSUOUS | | A. Pushed to one's emotional limits |
| W - 2. SOLIDIFIED | | B. Beginning to exist |
| L - 3. BEFUDDLED | | C. A state of alarm or dread |
| A - 4. OVERSTRUNG | | D. Settles something conclusively |
| Y - 5. IMPLACABLY | | E. To rid one's mind of |
| V - 6. CANDIDLY | | F. Enthusiastically; with great interest |
| D - 7. CLINCHES | | G. Likely; at risk of experiencing something unpleasant |
| B - 8. INCIPIENT | | H. Appealing to the senses |
| U - 9. PHILANDERING | | I. To say aloud to be recorded & then written by another from the recording |
| P - 10. LACONIC | | J. Threateningly |
| I - 11. DICTATION | | K. Made less intense; toned down; softened |
| J - 12. OMINOUSLY | | L. Confused |
| R - 13. OVEREMPHASIZE | | M. Rough-sounding; harsh; boisterous |
| C - 14. TREPIDATION | | N. Suffering great anguish; struggling |
| K - 15. SUBDUED | | O. Quick & changeable in temperament |
| T - 16. ENTHRALLED | | P. Using few words |
| N - 17. AGONIZED | | Q. Existing alone |
| E - 18. DISPEL | | R. Place too much importance on |
| G - 19. LIABLE | | S. Concentrating; engrossed |
| S - 20. INTENT | | T. Held spellbound; captivated |
| M - 21. RAUCOUS | | U. Engaging in many casual love affairs |
| Q - 22. SOLITARY | | V. Characterized by openness; frankly; straightforward |
| F - 23. AVIDLY | | W. Made strong, sturdy or stable |
| X - 24. COMRADESHIP | | X. Friendship; friendly spirit of working together |
| O - 25. MERCURIAL | | Y. In a manner showing unwillingness to make peace |

Death of a Salesman Vocabulary Matching 3

___ 1. SUBDUED  
___ 2. FALTERS  
___ 3. OVERSTRUNG  
___ 4. INCIPIENT  
___ 5. ANXIOUSLY  
___ 6. RAUCOUS  
___ 7. SOLIDIFIED  
___ 8. STRIVING  
___ 9. BEFUDDLED  
___ 10. COMRADESHIP  
___ 11. DICTATION  
___ 12. SOLITARY  
___ 13. PHILANDERING  
___ 14. REMISS  
___ 15. LACONIC  
___ 16. TREPIDATION  
___ 17. AVIDLY  
___ 18. CANDIDLY  
___ 19. DISPEL  
___ 20. IMITATED  
___ 21. INSINUATES  
___ 22. IMPLACABLY  
___ 23. GIST  
___ 24. MERCURIAL  
___ 25. INCARNATE  

A. To say aloud to be recorded & then written by another from the recording  
B. Main idea  
C. Made less intense; toned down; softened  
D. Becomes introduced gradually  
E. Personified; given a human form  
F. A state of alarm or dread  
G. Quick & changeable in temperament  
H. Existing alone  
I. Pushed to one's emotional limits  
J. Using few words  
K. Characterized by openness; frankly; straightforward  
L. Stumbles; moves unsteadily  
M. Beginning to exist  
N. To rid one's mind of  
O. Copied mannerisms, actions or speech  
P. With a worried eagerness  
Q. Made strong, sturdy or stable  
R. Confused  
S. Friendship; friendly spirit of working together  
T. In a manner showing unwillingness to make peace  
U. Engaging in many casual love affairs  
V. Enthusiastically; with great interest  
W. Not attending to duty; negligent; careless  
X. Struggling; working  
Y. Rough-sounding; harsh; boisterous

Death of a Salesman Vocabulary Matching 3 Answer Key

| | | |
|---|---|---|
| C - 1. SUBDUED | A. | To say aloud to be recorded & then written by another from the recording |
| L - 2. FALTERS | B. | Main idea |
| I - 3. OVERSTRUNG | C. | Made less intense; toned down; softened |
| M - 4. INCIPIENT | D. | Becomes introduced gradually |
| P - 5. ANXIOUSLY | E. | Personified; given a human form |
| Y - 6. RAUCOUS | F. | A state of alarm or dread |
| Q - 7. SOLIDIFIED | G. | Quick & changeable in temperament |
| X - 8. STRIVING | H. | Existing alone |
| R - 9. BEFUDDLED | I. | Pushed to one's emotional limits |
| S - 10. COMRADESHIP | J. | Using few words |
| A - 11. DICTATION | K. | Characterized by openness; frankly; straightforward |
| H - 12. SOLITARY | L. | Stumbles; moves unsteadily |
| U - 13. PHILANDERING | M. | Beginning to exist |
| W - 14. REMISS | N. | To rid one's mind of |
| J - 15. LACONIC | O. | Copied mannerisms, actions or speech |
| F - 16. TREPIDATION | P. | With a worried eagerness |
| V - 17. AVIDLY | Q. | Made strong, sturdy or stable |
| K - 18. CANDIDLY | R. | Confused |
| N - 19. DISPEL | S. | Friendship; friendly spirit of working together |
| O - 20. IMITATED | T. | In a manner showing unwillingness to make peace |
| D - 21. INSINUATES | U. | Engaging in many casual love affairs |
| T - 22. IMPLACABLY | V. | Enthusiastically; with great interest |
| B - 23. GIST | W. | Not attending to duty; negligent; careless |
| G - 24. MERCURIAL | X. | Struggling; working |
| E - 25. INCARNATE | Y. | Rough-sounding; harsh; boisterous |

Copyrighted

Death of a Salesman Vocabulary Matching 4

___ 1. REMISS              A. Not attending to duty; negligent; careless
___ 2. INTENT              B. Suffering great anguish; struggling
___ 3. MERCURIAL           C. Made strong, sturdy or stable
___ 4. SOLITARY            D. Using few words
___ 5. GIST                E. Dishonorable; disgraceful
___ 6. DICTATION           F. Likely; at risk of experiencing something unpleasant
___ 7. LACONIC             G. A state of alarm or dread
___ 8. BEFUDDLED           H. Quick & changeable in temperament
___ 9. INCREDULOUSLY       I. Main idea
___10. TREPIDATION         J. Friendship; friendly spirit of working together
___11. COMRADESHIP         K. Place too much importance on
___12. ANXIOUSLY           L. Appealing to the senses
___13. LIABLE              M. Enthusiastically; with great interest
___14. INCARNATE           N. Concentrating; engrossed
___15. SUBDUED             O. Threateningly
___16. CONTEMPTUOUS        P. Existing alone
___17. RAUCOUS             Q. With a worried eagerness
___18. SENSUOUS            R. Struggling; working
___19. AVIDLY              S. Made less intense; toned down; softened
___20. OMINOUSLY           T. Unbelievingly
___21. OVEREMPHASIZE       U. To say aloud to be recorded & then written by another from the recording
___22. AGONIZED            V. Tender, romantic or nostalgic feeling
___23. STRIVING            W. Rough-sounding; harsh; boisterous
___24. SENTIMENT           X. Personified; given a human form
___25. SOLIDIFIED          Y. Confused

Death of a Salesman Vocabulary Matching 4 Answer Key

| | | |
|---|---|---|
| A - 1. REMISS | A. | Not attending to duty; negligent; careless |
| N - 2. INTENT | B. | Suffering great anguish; struggling |
| H - 3. MERCURIAL | C. | Made strong, sturdy or stable |
| P - 4. SOLITARY | D. | Using few words |
| I - 5. GIST | E. | Dishonorable; disgraceful |
| U - 6. DICTATION | F. | Likely; at risk of experiencing something unpleasant |
| D - 7. LACONIC | G. | A state of alarm or dread |
| Y - 8. BEFUDDLED | H. | Quick & changeable in temperament |
| T - 9. INCREDULOUSLY | I. | Main idea |
| G - 10. TREPIDATION | J. | Friendship; friendly spirit of working together |
| J - 11. COMRADESHIP | K. | Place too much importance on |
| Q - 12. ANXIOUSLY | L. | Appealing to the senses |
| F - 13. LIABLE | M. | Enthusiastically; with great interest |
| X - 14. INCARNATE | N. | Concentrating; engrossed |
| S - 15. SUBDUED | O. | Threateningly |
| E - 16. CONTEMPTUOUS | P. | Existing alone |
| W - 17. RAUCOUS | Q. | With a worried eagerness |
| L - 18. SENSUOUS | R. | Struggling; working |
| M - 19. AVIDLY | S. | Made less intense; toned down; softened |
| O - 20. OMINOUSLY | T. | Unbelievingly |
| K - 21. OVEREMPHASIZE | U. | To say aloud to be recorded & then written by another from the recording |
| B - 22. AGONIZED | V. | Tender, romantic or nostalgic feeling |
| R - 23. STRIVING | W. | Rough-sounding; harsh; boisterous |
| V - 24. SENTIMENT | X. | Personified; given a human form |
| C - 25. SOLIDIFIED | Y. | Confused |

Death of a Salesman Vocabulary Magic Squares 1

Match the definition with the vocabulary word. Put your answers in the magic squares below. When your answers are correct, all columns and rows will add to the same number.

A. INSINUATES
B. SOLITARY
C. SENSUOUS
D. MERCURIAL
E. CLINCHES
F. INCREDULOUSLY
G. OMINOUSLY
H. DISPEL
I. INTENT
J. ENTHRALLED
K. LACONIC
L. TREPIDATION
M. FALTERS
N. GIST
O. IMITATED
P. COMRADESHIP

1. Existing alone
2. Threateningly
3. Using few words
4. Main idea
5. Stumbles; moves unsteadily
6. A state of alarm or dread
7. To rid one's mind of
8. Becomes introduced gradually
9. Friendship; friendly spirit of working together
10. Concentrating; engrossed
11. Settles something conclusively
12. Quick & changeable in temperament
13. Appealing to the senses
14. Unbelievingly
15. Held spellbound; captivated
16. Copied mannerisms, actions or speech

| A= | B= | C= | D= |
| E= | F= | G= | H= |
| I= | J= | K= | L= |
| M= | N= | O= | P= |

Death of a Salesman Vocabulary Magic Squares 1 Answer Key

Match the definition with the vocabulary word. Put your answers in the magic squares below. When your answers are correct, all columns and rows will add to the same number.

A. INSINUATES
B. SOLITARY
C. SENSUOUS
D. MERCURIAL
E. CLINCHES
F. INCREDULOUSLY
G. OMINOUSLY
H. DISPEL
I. INTENT
J. ENTHRALLED
K. LACONIC
L. TREPIDATION
M. FALTERS
N. GIST
O. IMITATED
P. COMRADESHIP

1. Existing alone
2. Threateningly
3. Using few words
4. Main idea
5. Stumbles; moves unsteadily
6. A state of alarm or dread
7. To rid one's mind of
8. Becomes introduced gradually
9. Friendship; friendly spirit of working together
10. Concentrating; engrossed
11. Settles something conclusively
12. Quick & changeable in temperament
13. Appealing to the senses
14. Unbelievingly
15. Held spellbound; captivated
16. Copied mannerisms, actions or speech

| A=8 | B=1 | C=13 | D=12 |
|---|---|---|---|
| E=11 | F=14 | G=2 | H=7 |
| I=10 | J=15 | K=3 | L=6 |
| M=5 | N=4 | O=16 | P=9 |

Death of a Salesman Vocabulary Magic Squares 2

Match the definition with the vocabulary word. Put your answers in the magic squares below. When your answers are correct, all columns and rows will add to the same number.

A. FALTERS
B. DICTATION
C. OVERSTRUNG
D. ENTHRALLED
E. IMPLACABLY
F. OVEREMPHASIZE
G. REMISS
H. DISPEL
I. MERCURIAL
J. INCIPIENT
K. SENTIMENT
L. SUBDUED
M. INCREDULOUSLY
N. INCARNATE
O. INTENT
P. STRIVING

1. Concentrating; engrossed
2. Beginning to exist
3. To rid one's mind of
4. Stumbles; moves unsteadily
5. Held spellbound; captivated
6. In a manner showing unwillingness to make peace
7. Tender, romantic or nostalgic feeling
8. Personified; given a human form
9. Place too much importance on
10. Pushed to one's emotional limits
11. Unbelievingly
12. Made less intense; toned down; softened
13. Quick & changeable in temperament
14. Struggling; working
15. To say aloud to be recorded & then written by another from the recording
16. Not attending to duty; negligent; careless

| A= | B= | C= | D= |
| --- | --- | --- | --- |
| E= | F= | G= | H= |
| I= | J= | K= | L= |
| M= | N= | O= | P= |

Death of a Salesman Vocabulary Magic Squares 2 Answer Key

Match the definition with the vocabulary word. Put your answers in the magic squares below. When your answers are correct, all columns and rows will add to the same number.

A. FALTERS
B. DICTATION
C. OVERSTRUNG
D. ENTHRALLED
E. IMPLACABLY
F. OVEREMPHASIZE
G. REMISS
H. DISPEL
I. MERCURIAL
J. INCIPIENT
K. SENTIMENT
L. SUBDUED
M. INCREDULOUSLY
N. INCARNATE
O. INTENT
P. STRIVING

1. Concentrating; engrossed
2. Beginning to exist
3. To rid one's mind of
4. Stumbles; moves unsteadily
5. Held spellbound; captivated
6. In a manner showing unwillingness to make peace
7. Tender, romantic or nostalgic feeling
8. Personified; given a human form
9. Place too much importance on
10. Pushed to one's emotional limits
11. Unbelievingly
12. Made less intense; toned down; softened
13. Quick & changeable in temperament
14. Struggling; working
15. To say aloud to be recorded & then written by another from the recording
16. Not attending to duty; negligent; careless

| A=4 | B=15 | C=10 | D=5 |
| --- | --- | --- | --- |
| E=6 | F=9 | G=16 | H=3 |
| I=13 | J=2 | K=7 | L=12 |
| M=11 | N=8 | O=1 | P=14 |

Death of a Salesman Vocabulary Magic Squares 3

Match the definition with the vocabulary word. Put your answers in the magic squares below. When your answers are correct, all columns and rows will add to the same number.

A. INCREDULOUSLY
B. OVEREMPHASIZE
C. PHILANDERING
D. INTENT
E. LACONIC
F. OMINOUSLY
G. IDEALIST
H. SENTIMENT
I. LIABLE
J. AGONIZED
K. MERCURIAL
L. AVIDLY
M. INCARNATE
N. IMPLACABLY
O. DICTATION
P. AGITATION

1. Unbelievingly
2. In a manner showing unwillingness to make peace
3. Suffering great anguish; struggling
4. Using few words
5. One who sees the best in things; a dreamer; not realistic
6. Enthusiastically; with great interest
7. Disturbance; annoyance
8. Engaging in many casual love affairs
9. To say aloud to be recorded & then written by another from the recording
10. Concentrating; engrossed
11. Tender, romantic or nostalgic feeling
12. Quick & changeable in temperament
13. Likely; at risk of experiencing something unpleasant
14. Threateningly
15. Place too much importance on
16. Personified; given a human form

| A= | B= | C= | D= |
|---|---|---|---|
| E= | F= | G= | H= |
| I= | J= | K= | L= |
| M= | N= | O= | P= |

Death of a Salesman Vocabulary Magic Squares 3 Answer Key

Match the definition with the vocabulary word. Put your answers in the magic squares below. When your answers are correct, all columns and rows will add to the same number.

A. INCREDULOUSLY
B. OVEREMPHASIZE
C. PHILANDERING
D. INTENT
E. LACONIC
F. OMINOUSLY
G. IDEALIST
H. SENTIMENT
I. LIABLE
J. AGONIZED
K. MERCURIAL
L. AVIDLY
M. INCARNATE
N. IMPLACABLY
O. DICTATION
P. AGITATION

1. Unbelievingly
2. In a manner showing unwillingness to make peace
3. Suffering great anguish; struggling
4. Using few words
5. One who sees the best in things; a dreamer; not realistic
6. Enthusiastically; with great interest
7. Disturbance; annoyance
8. Engaging in many casual love affairs
9. To say aloud to be recorded & then written by another from the recording
10. Concentrating; engrossed
11. Tender, romantic or nostalgic feeling
12. Quick & changeable in temperament
13. Likely; at risk of experiencing something unpleasant
14. Threateningly
15. Place too much importance on
16. Personified; given a human form

| A=1 | B=15 | C=8 | D=10 |
|---|---|---|---|
| E=4 | F=14 | G=5 | H=11 |
| I=13 | J=3 | K=12 | L=6 |
| M=16 | N=2 | O=9 | P=7 |

Death of a Salesman Vocabulary Magic Squares 4

Match the definition with the vocabulary word. Put your answers in the magic squares below. When your answers are correct, all columns and rows will add to the same number.

A. IMPLACABLY
B. TREPIDATION
C. BEFUDDLED
D. LIABLE
E. STRIVING
F. OMINOUSLY
G. INCREDULOUSLY
H. RAUCOUS
I. PHILANDERING
J. CANDIDLY
K. SUBDUED
L. ENTHRALLED
M. DISPEL
N. COMRADESHIP
O. LACONIC
P. REMISS

1. Rough-sounding; harsh; boisterous
2. To rid one's mind of
3. A state of alarm or dread
4. Made less intense; toned down; softened
5. Characterized by openness; frankly; straightforward
6. Confused
7. Not attending to duty; negligent; careless
8. Struggling; working
9. Using few words
10. Threateningly
11. Engaging in many casual love affairs
12. Likely; at risk of experiencing something unpleasant
13. In a manner showing unwillingness to make peace
14. Held spellbound; captivated
15. Unbelievingly
16. Friendship; friendly spirit of working together

| A= | B= | C= | D= |
| E= | F= | G= | H= |
| I= | J= | K= | L= |
| M= | N= | O= | P= |

Death of a Salesman Vocabulary Magic Squares 4 Answer Key

Match the definition with the vocabulary word. Put your answers in the magic squares below. When your answers are correct, all columns and rows will add to the same number.

A. IMPLACABLY
B. TREPIDATION
C. BEFUDDLED
D. LIABLE
E. STRIVING
F. OMINOUSLY
G. INCREDULOUSLY
H. RAUCOUS
I. PHILANDERING
J. CANDIDLY
K. SUBDUED
L. ENTHRALLED
M. DISPEL
N. COMRADESHIP
O. LACONIC
P. REMISS

1. Rough-sounding; harsh; boisterous
2. To rid one's mind of
3. A state of alarm or dread
4. Made less intense; toned down; softened
5. Characterized by openness; frankly; straightforward
6. Confused
7. Not attending to duty; negligent; careless
8. Struggling; working
9. Using few words
10. Threateningly
11. Engaging in many casual love affairs
12. Likely; at risk of experiencing something unpleasant
13. In a manner showing unwillingness to make peace
14. Held spellbound; captivated
15. Unbelievingly
16. Friendship; friendly spirit of working together

| A=13 | B=3 | C=6 | D=12 |
| --- | --- | --- | --- |
| E=8 | F=10 | G=15 | H=1 |
| I=11 | J=5 | K=4 | L=14 |
| M=2 | N=16 | O=9 | P=7 |

Death of a Salesman Vocabulary Word Search 1

Words are placed backwards, forward, diagonally, up and down. Clues listed below can help you find the words. Circle the hidden vocabulary words in the maze.

```
R F T S M E R C U R I A L K N T C H Y
E X M U K F Z S V H S Q P S N E O V D
M N N B T F A N S G R F F E D N N O N
I Y L D I V A L E L W T I H I T T V O
S R B U N O V K T T P D C C H E E I
S D N E C S M F A E I H E N T R M R T
N T B D A D Q I U C R L I A A P S A
S R E Y R Y I P N M G S F L T L T T T
T E F S N X N I I O J W I C I L U R I
R P U E A F T B S N U Q D Z O E O U G
I I D N T X E R N L H S I Y N D U N A
V D D T E A N X I O U S L Y K C S G L
I A L I W Y T A B X R B O Y D O O N R
N T E M Y G B C R B A L S E L N X D L
G I D E A L I S T C W U T I I G I S T
N O T N E N K M A N O A T Z X S H M D
K N R T O L T L V C T A E Z P G J K G
V H C C R Y P S U I R D K E V C Q W M
B N A T F M T A M Y X Y L D I D N A C
F L R X I T R I S E N S U O U S B K F
```

A state of alarm or dread (11)
Appealing to the senses (8)
Becomes introduced gradually (10)
Beginning to exist (9)
Characterized by openness; frankly; straightforward (8)
Concentrating; engrossed (6)
Confused (9)
Copied mannerisms, actions or speech (8)
Dishonorable; disgraceful (12)
Disturbance; annoyance (9)
Enthusiastically; with great interest (6)
Existing alone (8)
Held spellbound; captivated (10)
In a manner showing unwillingness to make peace (10)
Likely; at risk of experiencing something unpleasant (6)
Made less intense; toned down; softened (7)
Made strong, sturdy or stable (10)

Main idea (4)
Not attending to duty; negligent; careless (6)
One who sees the best in things; a dreamer; not realistic (8)
Personified; given a human form (9)
Pushed to one's emotional limits (10)
Quick & changeable in temperament (9)
Rough-sounding; harsh; boisterous (7)
Settles something conclusively (8)
Struggling; working (8)
Stumbles; moves unsteadily (7)
Suffering great anguish; struggling (8)
Tender, romantic or nostalgic feeling (9)
Threateningly (9)
To rid one's mind of (6)
To say aloud to be recorded & then written by another from the recording (9)
Using few words (7)
With a worried eagerness (9)

Death of a Salesman Vocabulary Word Search 1 Answer Key

Words are placed backwards, forward, diagonally, up and down. Clues listed below can help you find the words. Circle the hidden vocabulary words in the maze.

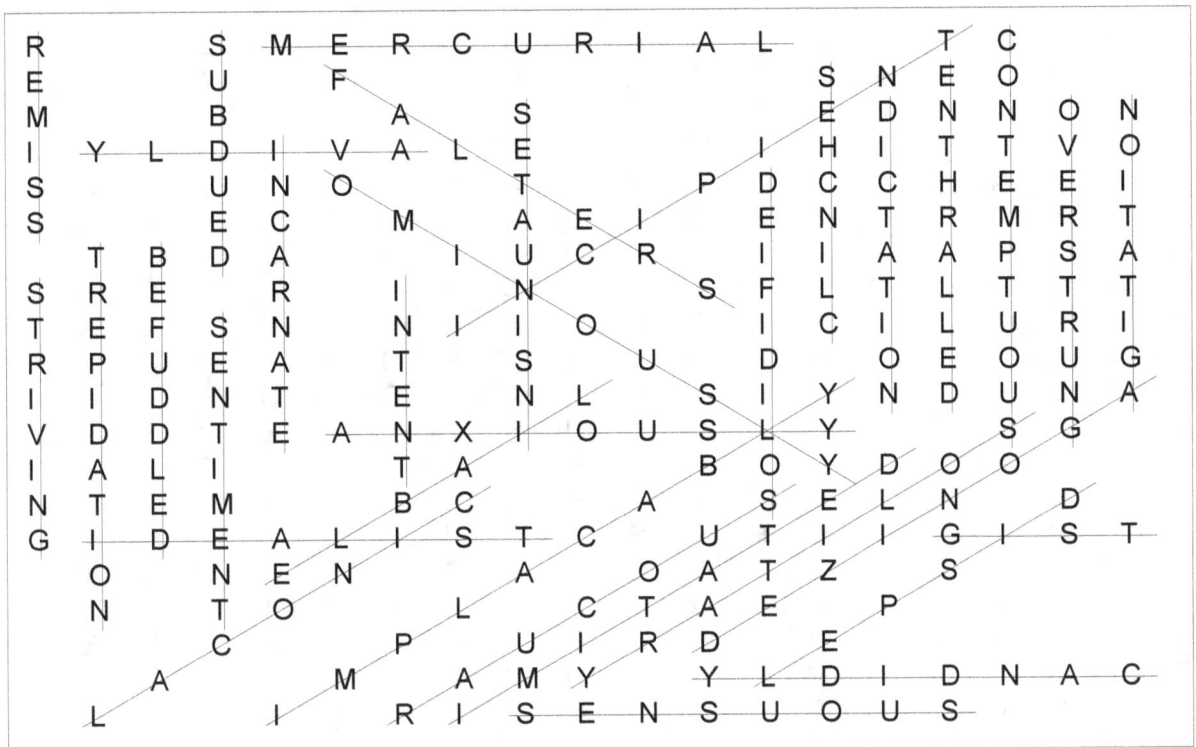

A state of alarm or dread (11)
Appealing to the senses (8)
Becomes introduced gradually (10)
Beginning to exist (9)
Characterized by openness; frankly; straightforward (8)
Concentrating; engrossed (6)
Confused (9)
Copied mannerisms, actions or speech (8)
Dishonorable; disgraceful (12)
Disturbance; annoyance (9)
Enthusiastically; with great interest (6)
Existing alone (8)
Held spellbound; captivated (10)
In a manner showing unwillingness to make peace (10)
Likely; at risk of experiencing something unpleasant (6)
Made less intense; toned down; softened (7)
Made strong, sturdy or stable (10)

Main idea (4)
Not attending to duty; negligent; careless (6)
One who sees the best in things; a dreamer; not realistic (8)
Personified; given a human form (9)
Pushed to one's emotional limits (10)
Quick & changeable in temperament (9)
Rough-sounding; harsh; boisterous (7)
Settles something conclusively (8)
Struggling; working (8)
Stumbles; moves unsteadily (7)
Suffering great anguish; struggling (8)
Tender, romantic or nostalgic feeling (9)
Threateningly (9)
To rid one's mind of (6)
To say aloud to be recorded & then written by another from the recording (9)
Using few words (7)
With a worried eagerness (9)

# Death of a Salesman Vocabulary Word Search 2

Words are placed backwards, forward, diagonally, up and down. Clues listed below can help you find the words. Circle the hidden vocabulary words in the maze.

```
C O N T E M P T U O U S A V I D L Y O
L X G T R E P I D A T I O N P E W Z V
N K I C S I N C A R N A T E H I G S E
L L S S S K J L O H F E F X I F G A R
V R T M M V A Y C V N X C S L I S N E
R S N C W C R J D T E D B K A D E X M
A V E H O A P I M K R R N F N I N I P
U Q S N T R W N I T C N S L D L T O H
C T I I S J B S G D B K R T E O I U A
O C L J Q U H I T E E M E Q R S M S S
U O D C P X O N F W R A T C I U E L I
S I N C R E D U L O U S L Y N Y N Y Z
S U S L M J D A S B B E A I G N T G E
I B B V Y D I T T P H F P S B V P Z Z
M T H D L R D E R S N C V N R T E P V
E W N E U L F S I C A N D I D L Y G M
R J D C S E X D V Q J I F Y B X F R G
P K R N V L D T I D E L L A R H T N E
D E T A T I M I N I C I P I E N T P
M N O I T A T I G A Y L S U O N I M O
```

A state of alarm or dread (11)
Appealing to the senses (8)
Becomes introduced gradually (10)
Beginning to exist (9)
Characterized by openness; frankly; straightforward (8)
Concentrating; engrossed (6)
Confused (9)
Copied mannerisms, actions or speech (8)
Dishonorable; disgraceful (12)
Disturbance; annoyance (9)
Engaging in many casual love affairs (12)
Enthusiastically; with great interest (6)
Existing alone (8)
Held spellbound; captivated (10)
Likely; at risk of experiencing something unpleasant (6)
Made less intense; toned down; softened (7)
Made strong, sturdy or stable (10)
Main idea (4)

Not attending to duty; negligent; careless (6)
One who sees the best in things; a dreamer; not realistic (8)
Personified; given a human form (9)
Place too much importance on (13)
Pushed to one's emotional limits (10)
Quick & changeable in temperament (9)
Rough-sounding; harsh; boisterous (7)
Settles something conclusively (8)
Struggling; working (8)
Stumbles; moves unsteadily (7)
Tender, romantic or nostalgic feeling (9)
Threateningly (9)
To rid one's mind of (6)
Unbelievingly (13)
Using few words (7)
With a worried eagerness (9)

Death of a Salesman Vocabulary Word Search 2 Answer Key

Words are placed backwards, forward, diagonally, up and down. Clues listed below can help you find the words. Circle the hidden vocabulary words in the maze.

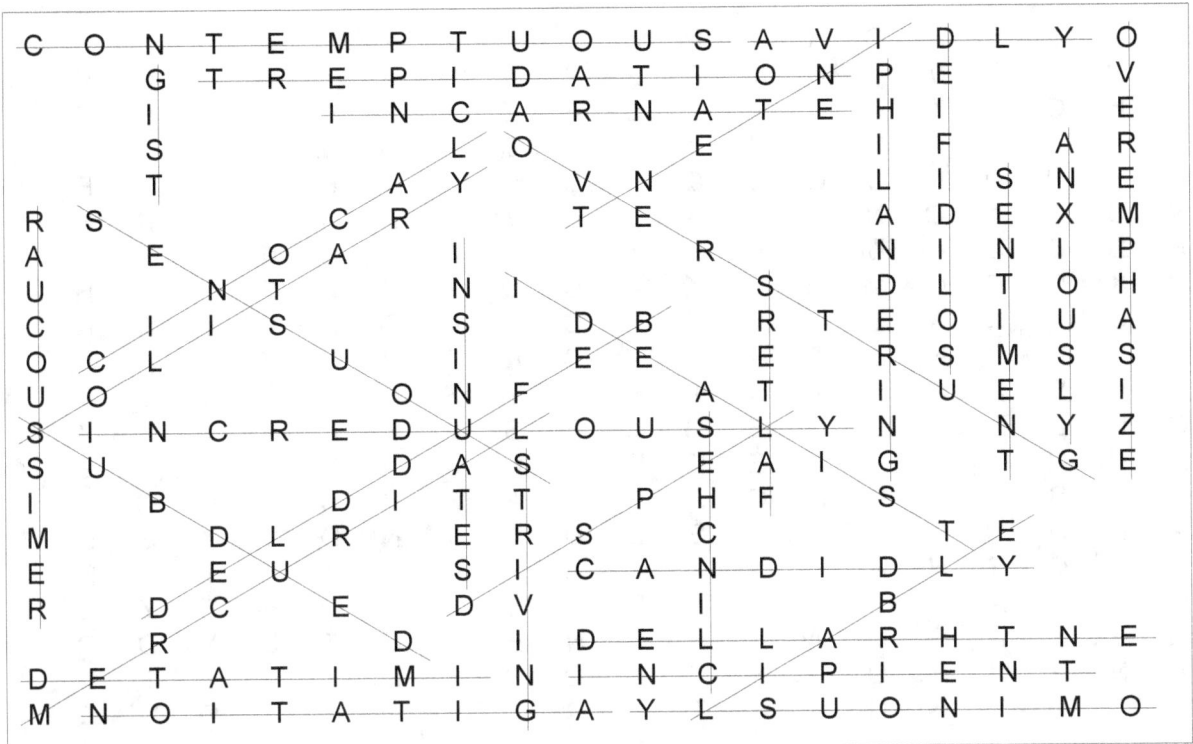

A state of alarm or dread (11)
Appealing to the senses (8)
Becomes introduced gradually (10)
Beginning to exist (9)
Characterized by openness; frankly; straightforward (8)
Concentrating; engrossed (6)
Confused (9)
Copied mannerisms, actions or speech (8)
Dishonorable; disgraceful (12)
Disturbance; annoyance (9)
Engaging in many casual love affairs (12)
Enthusiastically; with great interest (6)
Existing alone (8)
Held spellbound; captivated (10)
Likely; at risk of experiencing something unpleasant (6)
Made less intense; toned down; softened (7)
Made strong, sturdy or stable (10)
Main idea (4)

Not attending to duty; negligent; careless (6)
One who sees the best in things; a dreamer; not realistic (8)
Personified; given a human form (9)
Place too much importance on (13)
Pushed to one's emotional limits (10)
Quick & changeable in temperament (9)
Rough-sounding; harsh; boisterous (7)
Settles something conclusively (8)
Struggling; working (8)
Stumbles; moves unsteadily (7)
Tender, romantic or nostalgic feeling (9)
Threateningly (9)
To rid one's mind of (6)
Unbelievingly (13)
Using few words (7)
With a worried eagerness (9)

Death of a Salesman Vocabulary Word Search 3

Words are placed backwards, forward, diagonally, up and down. Words listed below are included in the maze. Circle the hidden vocabulary words in the maze.

```
I Y L B A C A L P M I J F F Q L H G O
K N A Z V T N T R E P I D A T I O N V
S H C C T F T A T S F E E I L A C I E
S E O A T C U Z Y O L Q T N M B A V R
I R N D R C O L Q L B N A T E L N I E
M C I T O N S M A I E W T E R E D R M
E B C U I U A R R T F F I N C G I T P
R K S F O M H T K A U Q M T U F D S H
Z C S N A T E G E R D L I G R E L R A
J H I D N L T N W Y D E B V I Z Y F S
N M S E C I T N T F L W S F A S J E I
O I E Z L D D E G D E S I H L X T F Z
I N N I I I E R H D D U X I A X T E
T C S N N C S G A S I A Z B U P G G F
A I U O C T P T S L D N V N D J X S L
T P O G H A E X O K I S I J U T Q F
I I U A E T L S P D H S X Y D R E Y C
G E S K S I W R P F N H T G F L X D R
A N P M F O A N X I O U S L Y L Y T V
Q T W P G N U R T S R E V O J L D W Q
```

| | | |
|---|---|---|
| AGITATION | GIST | OVEREMPHASIZE |
| AGONIZED | IDEALIST | OVERSTRUNG |
| ANXIOUSLY | IMITATED | RAUCOUS |
| AVIDLY | IMPLACABLY | REMISS |
| BEFUDDLED | INCARNATE | SENSUOUS |
| CANDIDLY | INCIPIENT | SENTIMENT |
| CLINCHES | INSINUATES | SOLIDIFIED |
| COMRADESHIP | INTENT | SOLITARY |
| DICTATION | LACONIC | STRIVING |
| DISPEL | LIABLE | SUBDUED |
| ENTHRALLED | MERCURIAL | TREPIDATION |
| FALTERS | OMINOUSLY | |

Death of a Salesman Vocabulary Word Search 3 Answer Key

Words are placed backwards, forward, diagonally, up and down. Words listed below are included in the maze. Circle the hidden vocabulary words in the maze.

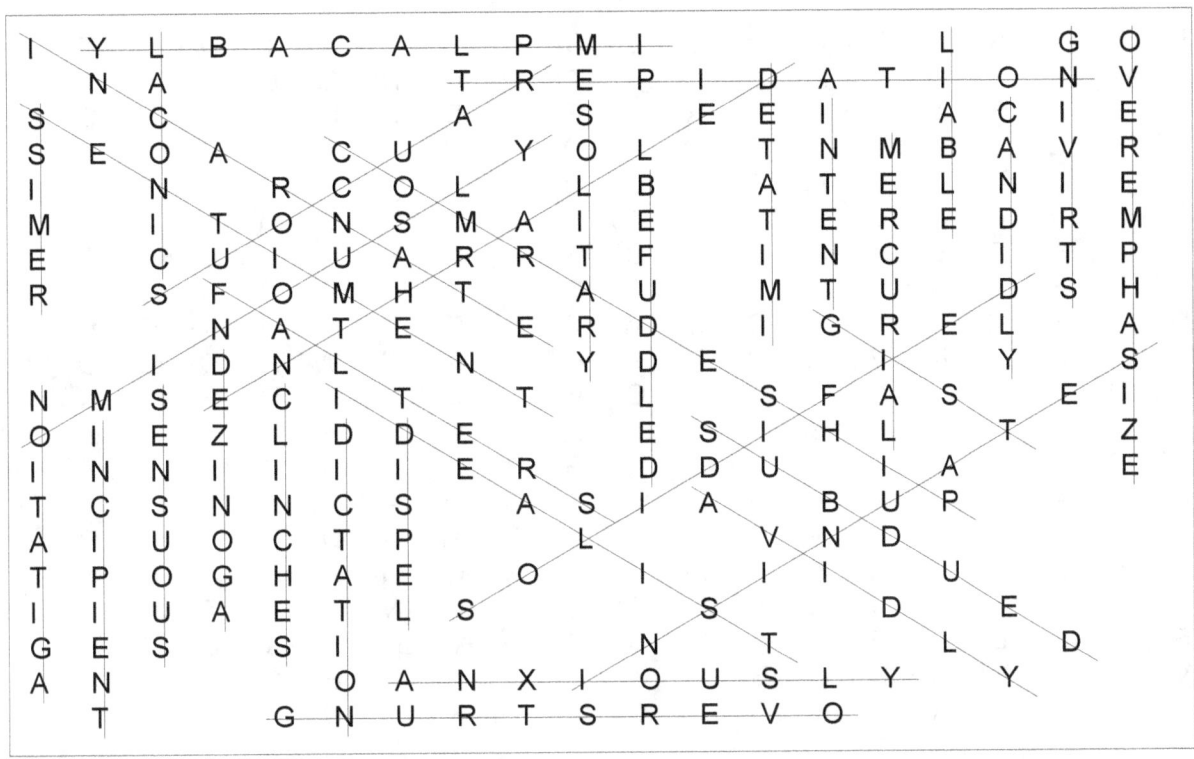

| AGITATION | GIST | OVEREMPHASIZE |
| AGONIZED | IDEALIST | OVERSTRUNG |
| ANXIOUSLY | IMITATED | RAUCOUS |
| AVIDLY | IMPLACABLY | REMISS |
| BEFUDDLED | INCARNATE | SENSUOUS |
| CANDIDLY | INCIPIENT | SENTIMENT |
| CLINCHES | INSINUATES | SOLIDIFIED |
| COMRADESHIP | INTENT | SOLITARY |
| DICTATION | LACONIC | STRIVING |
| DISPEL | LIABLE | SUBDUED |
| ENTHRALLED | MERCURIAL | TREPIDATION |
| FALTERS | OMINOUSLY | |

# Death of a Salesman Vocabulary Word Search 4

Words are placed backwards, forward, diagonally, up and down. Words listed below are included in the maze. Circle the hidden vocabulary words in the maze.

```
I N C R E D U L O U S L Y I A T M C T
O A P I D E A L I S T G R N G L B K R
V M N P N L Q N R T F T D C I V V Y E
E F G X G S Y P G Z Q N Y I T N P G P
R S O L I D I F I E D E F P A S H R I
S R R Q S O L N G J H M A I T U I A D
T S F B E B U N U C B I L E I B L U A
R R F Z H Q V S Y A G T T N O D A C T
U B E H C T A C L M T N E T N U N O I
N X D M N V M G B Y L E R T W E D U O
G D E Z I N O G A G V S S W M D E S N
K B L D L S B W C J B I O E E D R C Z
W G L Z C P S C A H G R R L C Y I D Z
D Y A G Q A T N L Z X C D A I H N N Y
S T R I V I N G P N U D M C D T G B R
P B H B D N X D M R U G C O I Z A P W
B Y T S F T R N I F L K G N S S T R S
S W N D Z E M A E D W J V I P X B G Y
V V E W H N L B V K L M S C E L T J M
I M I T A T E D Z G Y Y X E L B A I L
```

| AGITATION | IDEALIST | PHILANDERING |
| AGONIZED | IMITATED | RAUCOUS |
| ANXIOUSLY | IMPLACABLY | REMISS |
| AVIDLY | INCIPIENT | SENTIMENT |
| BEFUDDLED | INCREDULOUSLY | SOLIDIFIED |
| CANDIDLY | INSINUATES | SOLITARY |
| CLINCHES | INTENT | STRIVING |
| DISPEL | LACONIC | SUBDUED |
| ENTHRALLED | LIABLE | TREPIDATION |
| FALTERS | MERCURIAL | |
| GIST | OVERSTRUNG | |

Death of a Salesman Vocabulary Word Search 4 Answer Key

Words are placed backwards, forward, diagonally, up and down. Words listed below are included in the maze. Circle the hidden vocabulary words in the maze.

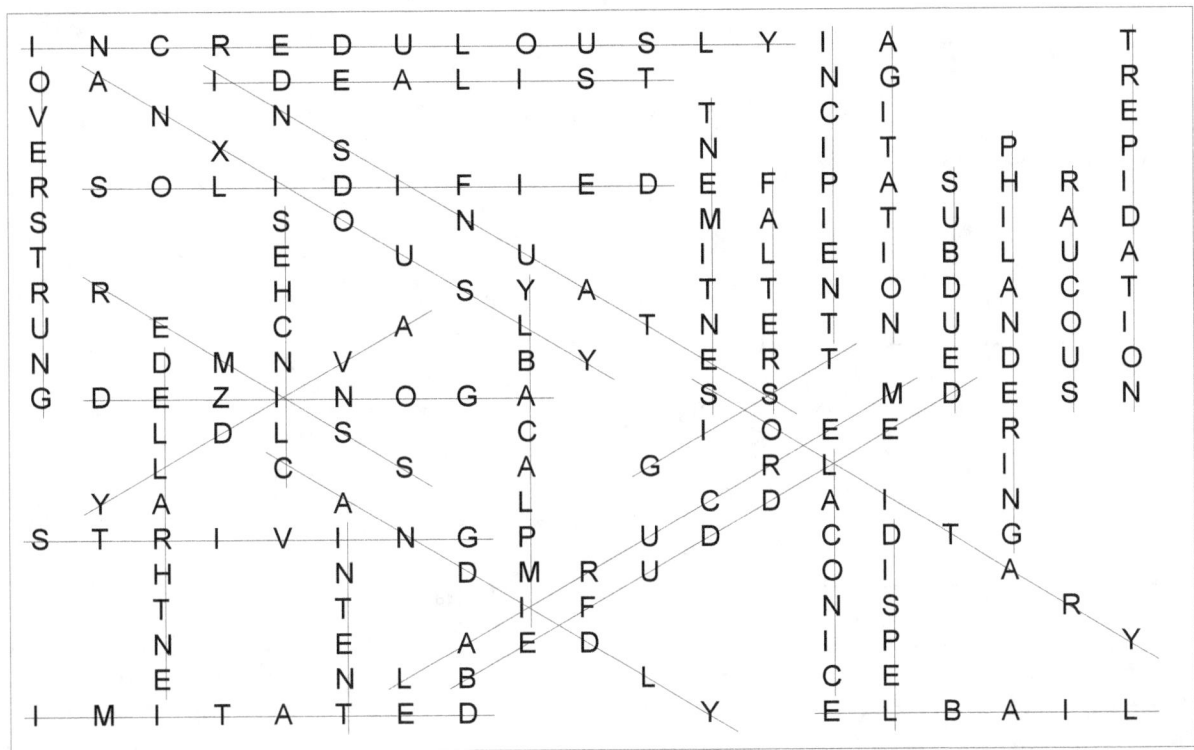

| AGITATION | IDEALIST | PHILANDERING |
| AGONIZED | IMITATED | RAUCOUS |
| ANXIOUSLY | IMPLACABLY | REMISS |
| AVIDLY | INCIPIENT | SENTIMENT |
| BEFUDDLED | INCREDULOUSLY | SOLIDIFIED |
| CANDIDLY | INSINUATES | SOLITARY |
| CLINCHES | INTENT | STRIVING |
| DISPEL | LACONIC | SUBDUED |
| ENTHRALLED | LIABLE | TREPIDATION |
| FALTERS | MERCURIAL | |
| GIST | OVERSTRUNG | |

Death of a Salesman Vocabulary Crossword 1

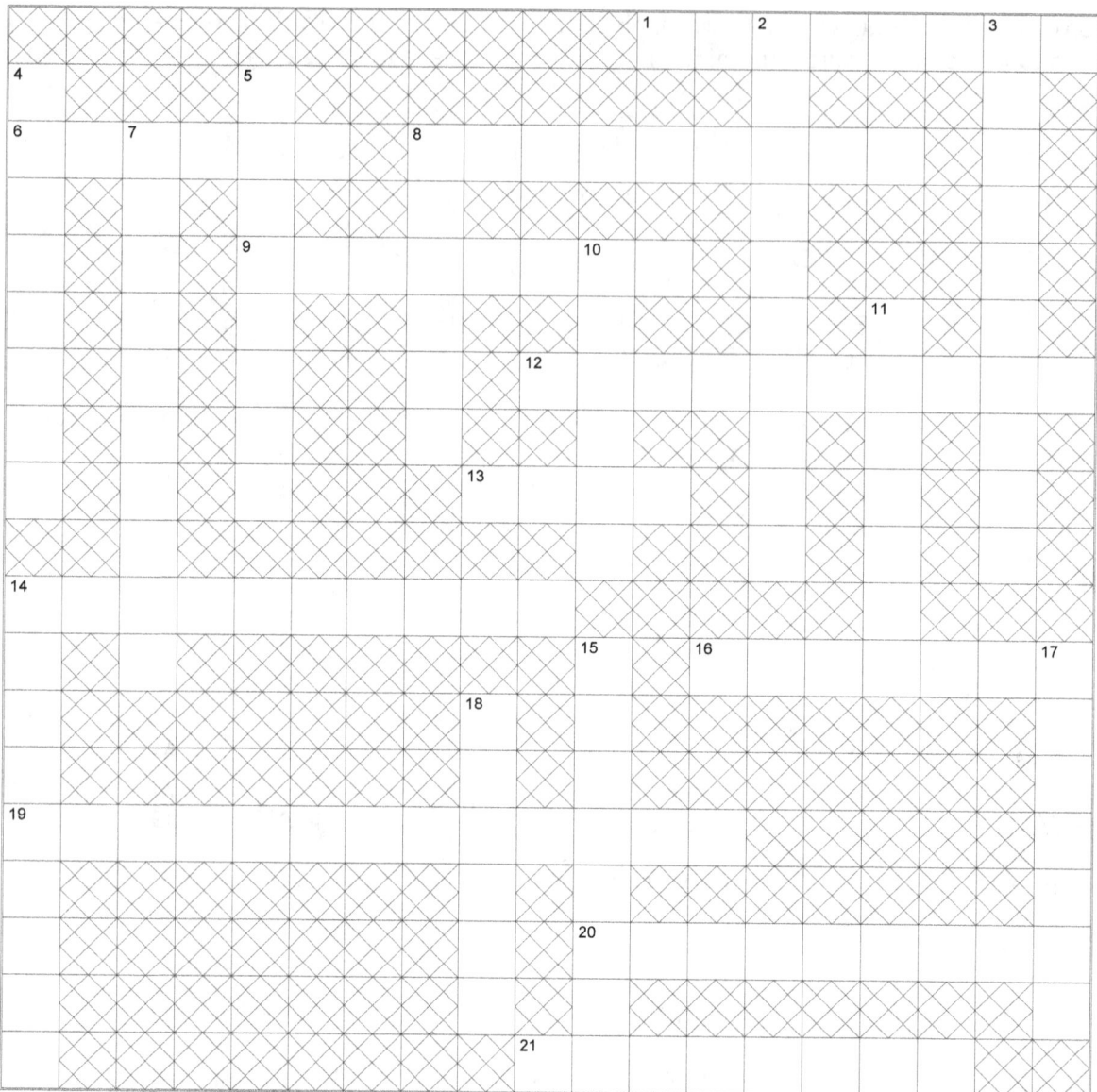

Across
1. Copied mannerisms, actions or speech
6. To rid one's mind of
8. With a worried eagerness
9. Existing alone
12. In a manner showing unwillingness to make peace
13. Main idea
14. Pushed to one's emotional limits
16. Rough-sounding; harsh; boisterous
19. Place too much importance on
20. Personified; given a human form
21. Suffering great anguish; struggling

Down
2. Becomes introduced gradually
3. Held spellbound; captivated
4. One who sees the best in things; a dreamer; not realistic
5. Appealing to the senses
7. Made strong, sturdy or stable
8. Enthusiastically; with great interest
10. Not attending to duty; negligent; careless
11. Using few words
14. Threateningly
15. Struggling; working
17. Made less intense; toned down; softened
18. Likely; at risk of experiencing something unpleasant

Death of a Salesman Vocabulary Crossword 1 Answer Key

Across
1. Copied mannerisms, actions or speech
6. To rid one's mind of
8. With a worried eagerness
9. Existing alone
12. In a manner showing unwillingness to make peace
13. Main idea
14. Pushed to one's emotional limits
16. Rough-sounding; harsh; boisterous
19. Place too much importance on
20. Personified; given a human form
21. Suffering great anguish; struggling

Down
2. Becomes introduced gradually
3. Held spellbound; captivated
4. One who sees the best in things; a dreamer; not realistic
5. Appealing to the senses
7. Made strong, sturdy or stable
8. Enthusiastically; with great interest
10. Not attending to duty; negligent; careless
11. Using few words
14. Threateningly
15. Struggling; working
17. Made less intense; toned down; softened
18. Likely; at risk of experiencing something unpleasant

# Death of a Salesman Vocabulary Crossword 2

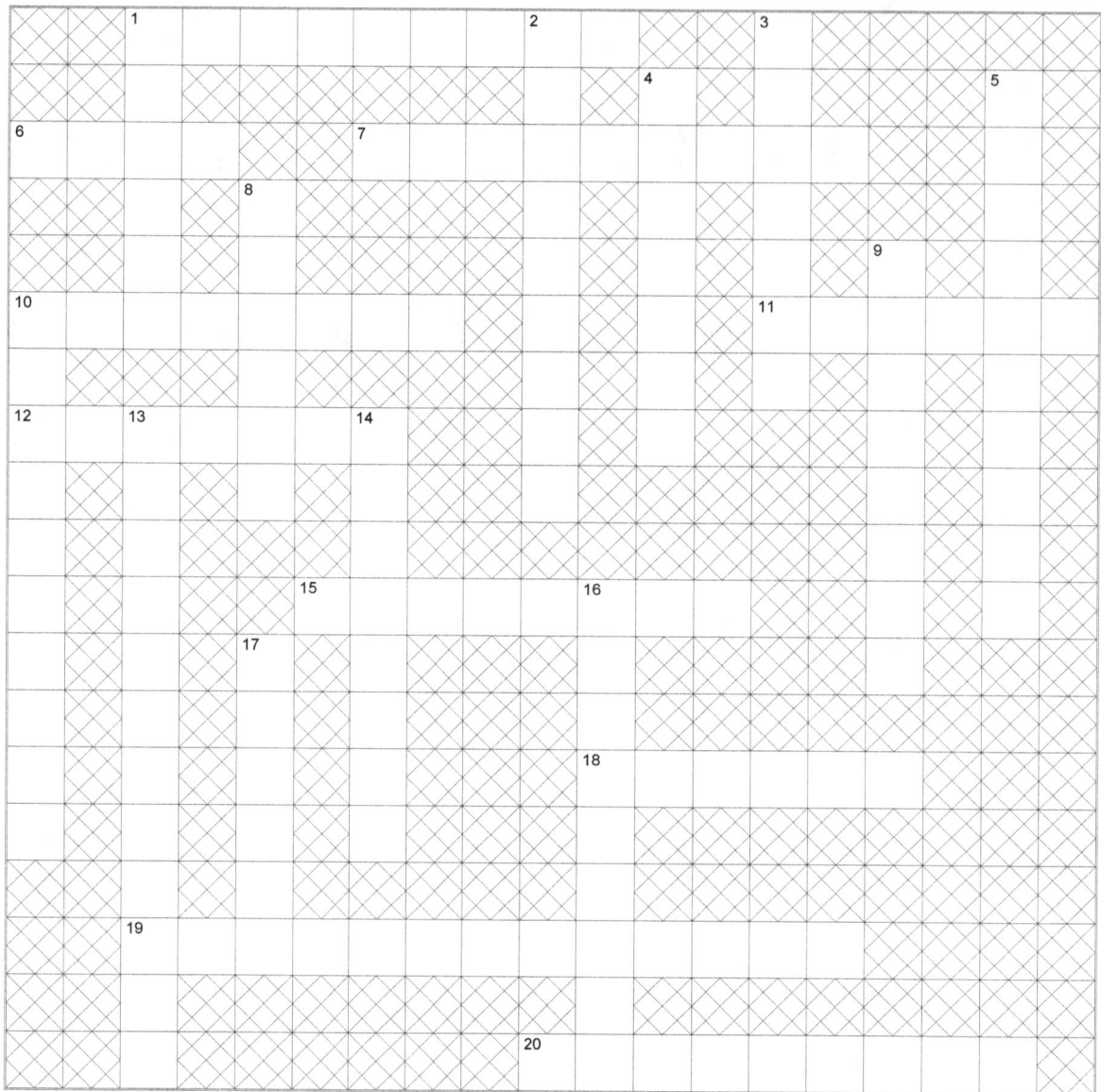

**Across**
1. To say aloud to be recorded & then written by another from the recording
6. Main idea
7. With a worried eagerness
10. Existing alone
11. Not attending to duty; negligent; careless
12. Using few words
15. One who sees the best in things; a dreamer; not realistic
18. Enthusiastically; with great interest
19. Place too much importance on
20. Confused

**Down**
1. To rid one's mind of
2. Threateningly
3. Stumbles; moves unsteadily
4. Made less intense; toned down; softened
5. Pushed to one's emotional limits
8. Concentrating; engrossed
9. Copied mannerisms, actions or speech
10. Made strong, sturdy or stable
13. Dishonorable; disgraceful
14. Characterized by openness; frankly; straightforward
16. Personified; given a human form
17. Likely; at risk of experiencing something unpleasant

# Death of a Salesman Vocabulary Crossword 2 Answer Key

**Across**
1. To say aloud to be recorded & then written by another from the recording
6. Main idea
7. With a worried eagerness
10. Existing alone
11. Not attending to duty; negligent; careless
12. Using few words
15. One who sees the best in things; a dreamer; not realistic
18. Enthusiastically; with great interest
19. Place too much importance on
20. Confused

**Down**
1. To rid one's mind of
2. Threateningly
3. Stumbles; moves unsteadily
4. Made less intense; toned down; softened
5. Pushed to one's emotional limits
8. Concentrating; engrossed
9. Copied mannerisms, actions or speech
10. Made strong, sturdy or stable
13. Dishonorable; disgraceful
14. Characterized by openness; frankly; straightforward
16. Personified; given a human form
17. Likely; at risk of experiencing something unpleasant

Death of a Salesman Vocabulary Crossword 3

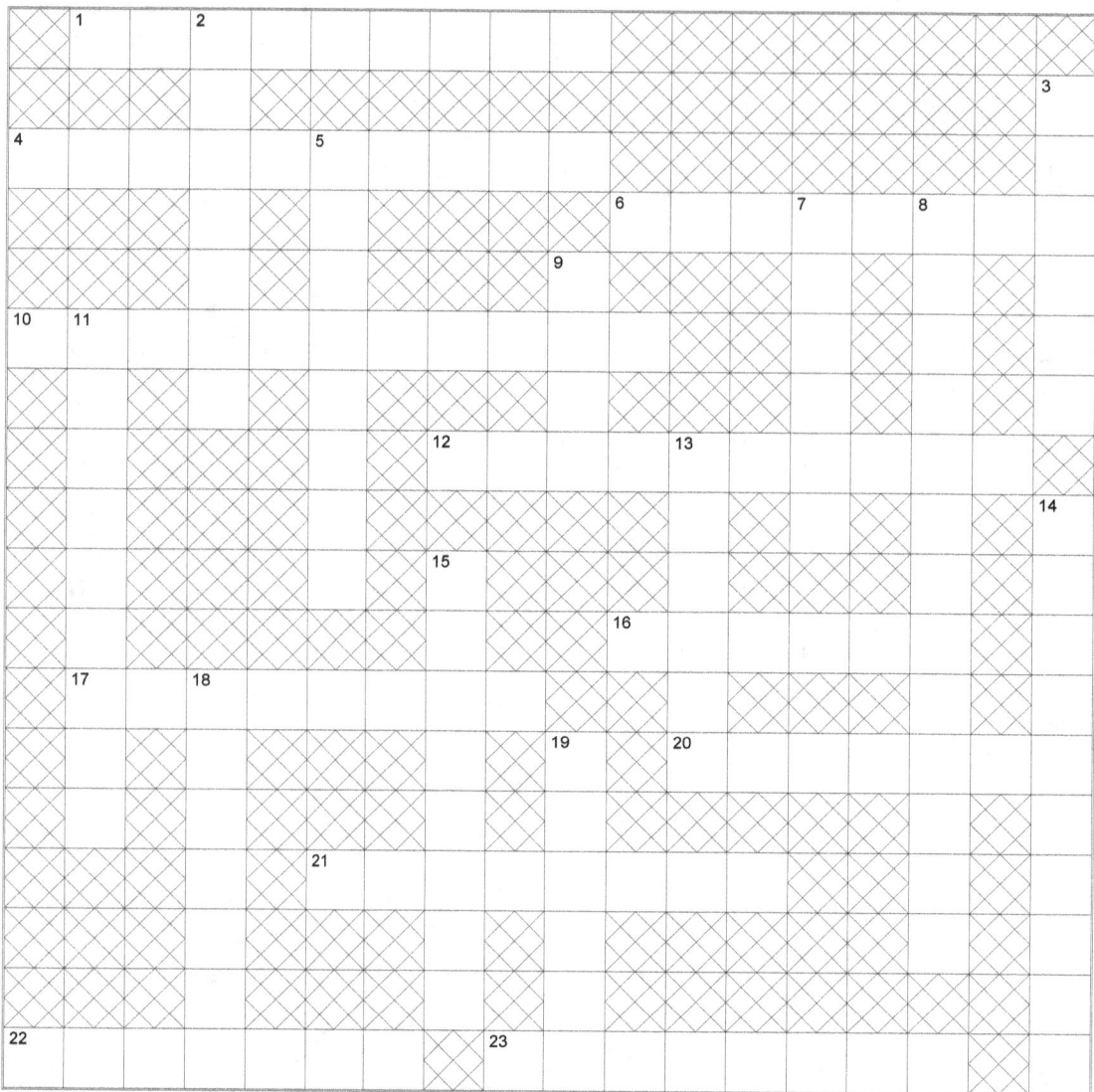

Across
1. Confused
4. In a manner showing unwillingness to make peace
6. One who sees the best in things; a dreamer; not realistic
10. Friendship; friendly spirit of working together
12. Held spellbound; captivated
16. To rid one's mind of
17. Existing alone
20. Made less intense; toned down; softened
21. Copied mannerisms, actions or speech
22. Rough-sounding; harsh; boisterous
23. Appealing to the senses

Down
2. Stumbles; moves unsteadily
3. Concentrating; engrossed
5. Characterized by openness; frankly; straightforward
7. Enthusiastically; with great interest
8. Unbelievingly
9. Main idea
11. Threateningly
13. Not attending to duty; negligent; careless
14. Made strong, sturdy or stable
15. Struggling; working
18. Using few words
19. Likely; at risk of experiencing something unpleasant

Death of a Salesman Vocabulary Crossword 3 Answer Key

**Across**
1. Confused
4. In a manner showing unwillingness to make peace
6. One who sees the best in things; a dreamer; not realistic
10. Friendship; friendly spirit of working together
12. Held spellbound; captivated
16. To rid one's mind of
17. Existing alone
20. Made less intense; toned down; softened
21. Copied mannerisms, actions or speech
22. Rough-sounding; harsh; boisterous
23. Appealing to the senses

**Down**
2. Stumbles; moves unsteadily
3. Concentrating; engrossed
5. Characterized by openness; frankly; straightforward
7. Enthusiastically; with great interest
8. Unbelievingly
9. Main idea
11. Threateningly
13. Not attending to duty; negligent; careless
14. Made strong, sturdy or stable
15. Struggling; working
18. Using few words
19. Likely; at risk of experiencing something unpleasant

Death of a Salesman Vocabulary Crossword 4

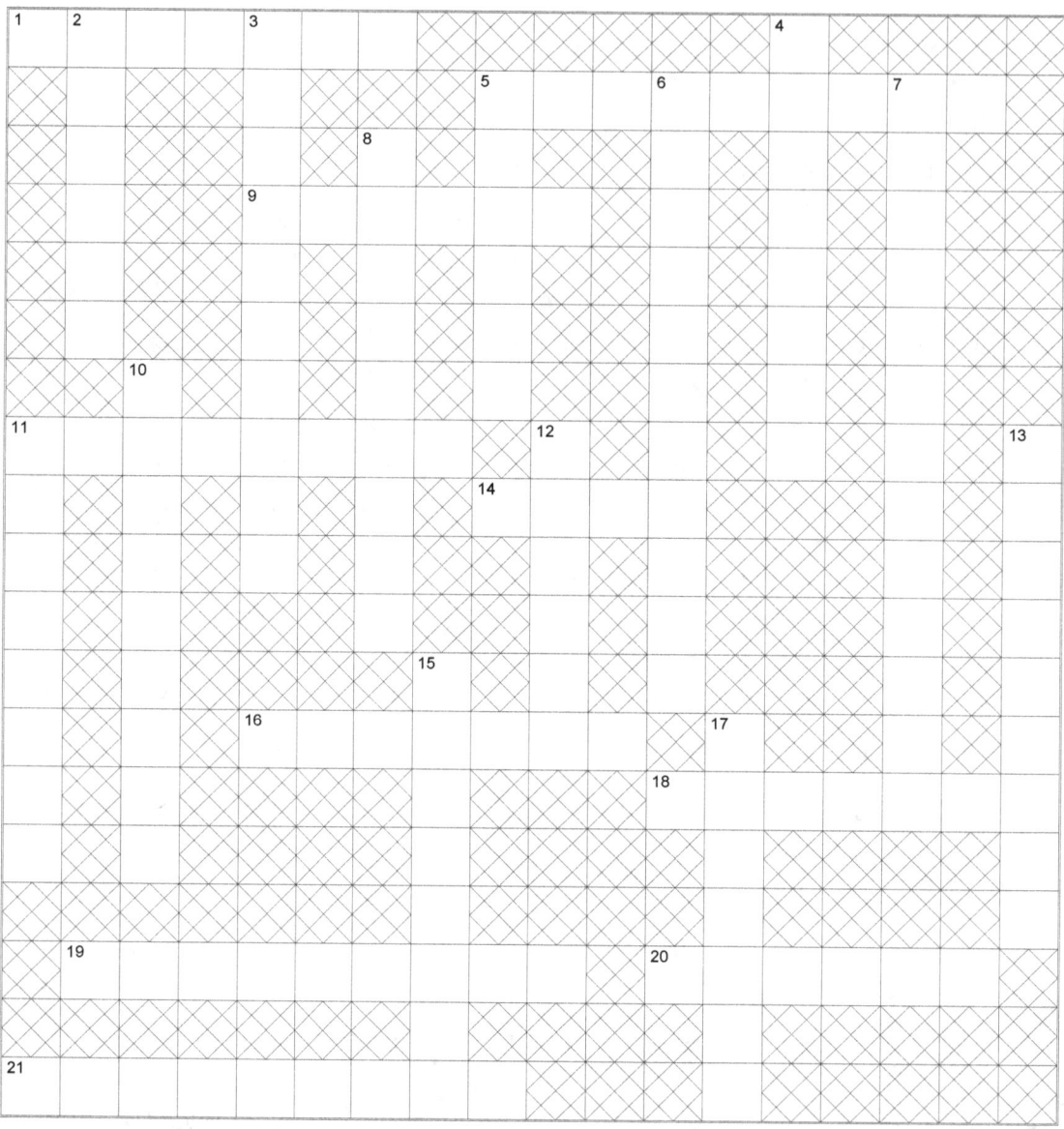

**Across**
1. Rough-sounding; harsh; boisterous
5. To say aloud to be recorded & then written by another from the recording
9. Not attending to duty; negligent; careless
11. Appealing to the senses
14. Main idea
16. Made less intense; toned down; softened
18. Stumbles; moves unsteadily
19. Disturbance; annoyance
20. Concentrating; engrossed
21. Personified; given a human form

**Down**
2. Enthusiastically; with great interest
3. Pushed to one's emotional limits
4. Struggling; working
5. To rid one's mind of
6. A state of alarm or dread
7. Place too much importance on
8. Threateningly
10. Beginning to exist
11. Existing alone
12. Likely; at risk of experiencing something unpleasant
13. With a worried eagerness
15. One who sees the best in things; a dreamer; not realistic
17. Using few words

# Death of a Salesman Vocabulary Crossword 4 Answer Key

**Across**
1. Rough-sounding; harsh; boisterous
5. To say aloud to be recorded & then written by another from the recording
9. Not attending to duty; negligent; careless
11. Appealing to the senses
14. Main idea
16. Made less intense; toned down; softened
18. Stumbles; moves unsteadily
19. Disturbance; annoyance
20. Concentrating; engrossed
21. Personified; given a human form

**Down**
2. Enthusiastically; with great interest
3. Pushed to one's emotional limits
4. Struggling; working
5. To rid one's mind of
6. A state of alarm or dread
7. Place too much importance on
8. Threateningly
10. Beginning to exist
11. Existing alone
12. Likely; at risk of experiencing something unpleasant
13. With a worried eagerness
15. One who sees the best in things; a dreamer; not realistic
17. Using few words

**Answers in grid:**

- 1 Across: RAUCOUS
- 5 Across: DICTATION
- 9 Across: REMISS
- 11 Across: SENSUOUS
- 14 Across: GIST
- 16 Across: SUBDUED
- 18 Across: FALTERS
- 19 Across: AGITATION
- 20 Across: INTENT
- 21 Across: INCARNATE
- 2 Down: AVIDLY
- 3 Down: OVERWROUGHT
- 4 Down: STRIVING
- 5 Down: DISPEL
- 6 Down: TREPIDATION
- 7 Down: OVEREMPHASIZE
- 8 Down: OMINOUSLY
- 10 Down: INCIPIENT
- 11 Down: SOLITARY
- 12 Down: LIABLE
- 13 Down: ANXIOUSLY
- 15 Down: IDEALIST
- 17 Down: LACONIC

Death of a Salesman Vocabulary Juggle Letters 1

1. IBLLEA = 1. _____
   Likely; at risk of experiencing something unpleasant

2. SIOUOMLNY = 2. _____
   Threateningly

3. UDDBUES = 3. _____
   Made less intense; toned down; softened

4. COURUSA = 4. _____
   Rough-sounding; harsh; boisterous

5. OTRIIANETDP = 5. _____
   A state of alarm or dread

6. OUONEUTSCMTP = 6. _____
   Dishonorable; disgraceful

7. IATIGATON = 7. _____
   Disturbance; annoyance

8. RIHEPOASDMC = 8. _____
   Friendship; friendly spirit of working together

9. INSUTSIAEN = 9. _____
   Becomes introduced gradually

10. SIIDFLOEDI =10. _____
    Made strong, sturdy or stable

11. RNDTHEALEL =11. _____
    Held spellbound; captivated

12. EIADSTLI =12. _____
    One who sees the best in things; a dreamer; not realistic

13. TIEMSNETN =13. _____
    Tender, romantic or nostalgic feeling

14. XLAYNOUSI =14. _____
    With a worried eagerness

15. NTCIOIADT =15. _____
    To say aloud to be recorded & then written by another from the recording

Death of a Salesman Vocabulary Juggle Letters 1 Answer Key

1. IBLLEA = 1. LIABLE
Likely; at risk of experiencing something unpleasant

2. SIOUOMLNY = 2. OMINOUSLY
Threateningly

3. UDDBUES = 3. SUBDUED
Made less intense; toned down; softened

4. COURUSA = 4. RAUCOUS
Rough-sounding; harsh; boisterous

5. OTRIIANETDP = 5. TREPIDATION
A state of alarm or dread

6. OUONEUTSCMTP = 6. CONTEMPTUOUS
Dishonorable; disgraceful

7. IATIGATON = 7. AGITATION
Disturbance; annoyance

8. RIHEPOASDMC = 8. COMRADESHIP
Friendship; friendly spirit of working together

9. INSUTSIAEN = 9. INSINUATES
Becomes introduced gradually

10. SIIDFLOEDI = 10. SOLIDIFIED
Made strong, sturdy or stable

11. RNDTHEALEL = 11. ENTHRALLED
Held spellbound; captivated

12. EIADSTLI = 12. IDEALIST
One who sees the best in things; a dreamer; not realistic

13. TIEMSNETN = 13. SENTIMENT
Tender, romantic or nostalgic feeling

14. XLAYNOUSI = 14. ANXIOUSLY
With a worried eagerness

15. NTCIOIADT = 15. DICTATION
To say aloud to be recorded & then written by another from the recording

Death of a Salesman Vocabulary Juggle Letters 2

1. ALPLACYMIB = 1. _____
In a manner showing unwillingness to make peace

2. AEITNUSISN = 2. _____
Becomes introduced gradually

3. VOAPEZISEEHMR = 3. _____
Place too much importance on

4. NTITEN = 4. _____
Concentrating; engrossed

5. SSMEIR = 5. _____
Not attending to duty; negligent; careless

6. DMCHOSIPEAR = 6. _____
Friendship; friendly spirit of working together

7. NGAODZEI = 7. _____
Suffering great anguish; struggling

8. RLHADNETEL = 8. _____
Held spellbound; captivated

9. OEUSUNSS = 9. _____
Appealing to the senses

10. LTSAOIYR = 10. _____
Existing alone

11. TAEIIDTM = 11. _____
Copied mannerisms, actions or speech

12. TISG = 12. _____
Main idea

13. IYMSONLOU = 13. _____
Threateningly

14. NCOALCI = 14. _____
Using few words

15. FDEEULBDD = 15. _____
Confused

Death of a Salesman Vocabulary Juggle Letters 2 Answer Key

1. ALPLACYMIB = 1. IMPLACABLY
   In a manner showing unwillingness to make peace

2. AEITNUSISN = 2. INSINUATES
   Becomes introduced gradually

3. VOAPEZISEEHMR = 3. OVEREMPHASIZE
   Place too much importance on

4. NTITEN = 4. INTENT
   Concentrating; engrossed

5. SSMEIR = 5. REMISS
   Not attending to duty; negligent; careless

6. DMCHOSIPEAR = 6. COMRADESHIP
   Friendship; friendly spirit of working together

7. NGAODZEI = 7. AGONIZED
   Suffering great anguish; struggling

8. RLHADNETEL = 8. ENTHRALLED
   Held spellbound; captivated

9. OEUSUNSS = 9. SENSUOUS
   Appealing to the senses

10. LTSAOIYR =10. SOLITARY
    Existing alone

11. TAEIIDTM =11. IMITATED
    Copied mannerisms, actions or speech

12. TISG =12. GIST
    Main idea

13. IYMSONLOU =13. OMINOUSLY
    Threateningly

14. NCOALCI =14. LACONIC
    Using few words

15. FDEEULBDD =15. BEFUDDLED
    Confused

Death of a Salesman Vocabulary Juggle Letters 3

1. CINIADOTT = 1. _____
To say aloud to be recorded & then written by another from the recording

2. NRPNLAIHDIEG = 2. _____
Engaging in many casual love affairs

3. ISSRME = 3. _____
Not attending to duty; negligent; careless

4. UUASCRO = 4. _____
Rough-sounding; harsh; boisterous

5. ZHSEOVRIPMAEE = 5. _____
Place too much importance on

6. TGIAONITA = 6. _____
Disturbance; annoyance

7. OFLIEIDSID = 7. _____
Made strong, sturdy or stable

8. ROYSLIAT = 8. _____
Existing alone

9. EINCTINIP = 9. _____
Beginning to exist

10. TELSIAID = 10. _____
One who sees the best in things; a dreamer; not realistic

11. YCNUELDOUSRLI = 11. _____
Unbelievingly

12. CALPAYBMIL = 12. _____
In a manner showing unwillingness to make peace

13. IBALLE = 13. _____
Likely; at risk of experiencing something unpleasant

14. DUSDEUB = 14. _____
Made less intense; toned down; softened

15. ULIONAYXS = 15. _____
With a worried eagerness

Death of a Salesman Vocabulary Juggle Letters 3 Answer Key

1. CINIADOTT = 1. DICTATION
   To say aloud to be recorded & then written by another from the recording

2. NRPNLAIHDIEG = 2. PHILANDERING
   Engaging in many casual love affairs

3. ISSRME = 3. REMISS
   Not attending to duty; negligent; careless

4. UUASCRO = 4. RAUCOUS
   Rough-sounding; harsh; boisterous

5. ZHSEOVRIPMAEE = 5. OVEREMPHASIZE
   Place too much importance on

6. TGIAONITA = 6. AGITATION
   Disturbance; annoyance

7. OFLIEIDSID = 7. SOLIDIFIED
   Made strong, sturdy or stable

8. ROYSLIAT = 8. SOLITARY
   Existing alone

9. EINCTINIP = 9. INCIPIENT
   Beginning to exist

10. TELSIAID = 10. IDEALIST
    One who sees the best in things; a dreamer; not realistic

11. YCNUELDOUSRLI = 11. INCREDULOUSLY
    Unbelievingly

12. CALPAYBMIL = 12. IMPLACABLY
    In a manner showing unwillingness to make peace

13. IBALLE = 13. LIABLE
    Likely; at risk of experiencing something unpleasant

14. DUSDEUB = 14. SUBDUED
    Made less intense; toned down; softened

15. ULIONAYXS = 15. ANXIOUSLY
    With a worried eagerness

Death of a Salesman Vocabulary Juggle Letters 4

1. AGIITOTNA = 1. _____
   Disturbance; annoyance

2. YXLOINSUA = 2. _____
   With a worried eagerness

3. TRGNIISV = 3. _____
   Struggling; working

4. NIIPINCET = 4. _____
   Beginning to exist

5. NCAOCIL = 5. _____
   Using few words

6. MTATIDEI = 6. _____
   Copied mannerisms, actions or speech

7. PTNOTOMCSUEU = 7. _____
   Dishonorable; disgraceful

8. TENETMSNI = 8. _____
   Tender, romantic or nostalgic feeling

9. UAURCSO = 9. _____
   Rough-sounding; harsh; boisterous

10. MHZVOESAREEPI =10. _____
    Place too much importance on

11. UIOSMYLNO =11. _____
    Threateningly

12. EUDUSDB =12. _____
    Made less intense; toned down; softened

13. SAIDELTI =13. _____
    One who sees the best in things; a dreamer; not realistic

14. TUIENINSSA =14. _____
    Becomes introduced gradually

15. SEIPLD =15. _____
    To rid one's mind of

Death of a Salesman Vocabulary Juggle Letters 4 Answer Key

1. AGIITOTNA = 1. AGITATION
Disturbance; annoyance

2. YXLOINSUA = 2. ANXIOUSLY
With a worried eagerness

3. TRGNIISV = 3. STRIVING
Struggling; working

4. NIIPINCET = 4. INCIPIENT
Beginning to exist

5. NCAOCIL = 5. LACONIC
Using few words

6. MTATIDEI = 6. IMITATED
Copied mannerisms, actions or speech

7. PTNOTOMCSUEU = 7. CONTEMPTUOUS
Dishonorable; disgraceful

8. TENETMSNI = 8. SENTIMENT
Tender, romantic or nostalgic feeling

9. UAURCSO = 9. RAUCOUS
Rough-sounding; harsh; boisterous

10. MHZVOESAREEPI = 10. OVEREMPHASIZE
Place too much importance on

11. UIOSMYLNO = 11. OMINOUSLY
Threateningly

12. EUDUSDB = 12. SUBDUED
Made less intense; toned down; softened

13. SAIDELTI = 13. IDEALIST
One who sees the best in things; a dreamer; not realistic

14. TUIENINSSA = 14. INSINUATES
Becomes introduced gradually

15. SEIPLD = 15. DISPEL
To rid one's mind of

| | |
|---|---|
| AGITATION | Disturbance; annoyance |
| AGONIZED | Suffering great anguish; struggling |
| ANXIOUSLY | With a worried eagerness |
| AVIDLY | Enthusiastically; with great interest |
| BEFUDDLED | Confused |
| CANDIDLY | Characterized by openness; frankly; straightforward |

| | |
|---|---|
| CLINCHES | Settles something conclusively |
| COMRADESHIP | Friendship; friendly spirit of working together |
| CONTEMPTUOUS | Dishonorable; disgraceful |
| DICTATION | To say aloud to be recorded & then written by another from the recording |
| DISPEL | To rid one's mind of |
| ENTHRALLED | Held spellbound; captivated |

| | |
|---|---|
| FALTERS | Stumbles; moves unsteadily |
| GIST | Main idea |
| IDEALIST | One who sees the best in things; a dreamer; not realistic |
| IMITATED | Copied mannerisms, actions or speech |
| IMPLACABLY | In a manner showing unwillingness to make peace |
| INCARNATE | Personified; given a human form |

| | |
|---|---|
| INCIPIENT | Beginning to exist |
| INCREDULOUSLY | Unbelievingly |
| INSINUATES | Becomes introduced gradually |
| INTENT | Concentrating; engrossed |
| LACONIC | Using few words |
| LIABLE | Likely; at risk of experiencing something unpleasant |

| | |
|---|---|
| MERCURIAL | Quick & changeable in temperament |
| OMINOUSLY | Threateningly |
| OVEREMPHASIZE | Place too much importance on |
| OVERSTRUNG | Pushed to one's emotional limits |
| PHILANDERING | Engaging in many casual love affairs |
| RAUCOUS | Rough-sounding; harsh; boisterous |

| | |
|---|---|
| REMISS | Not attending to duty; negligent; careless |
| SENSUOUS | Appealing to the senses |
| SENTIMENT | Tender, romantic or nostalgic feeling |
| SOLIDIFIED | Made strong, sturdy or stable |
| SOLITARY | Existing alone |
| STRIVING | Struggling; working |

| SUBDUED | Made less intense; toned down; softened |
|---|---|
| TREPIDATION | A state of alarm or dread |
| | |
| | |
| | |

Death of a Salesman Vocabulary

| BEFUDDLED | OMINOUSLY | RAUCOUS | LACONIC | SENSUOUS |
|---|---|---|---|---|
| FALTERS | DISPEL | INCIPIENT | SOLITARY | SENTIMENT |
| ENTHRALLED | INCREDULOUSLY | FREE SPACE | LIABLE | DICTATION |
| INTENT | REMISS | CANDIDLY | CONTEMPTUOUS | IDEALIST |
| IMITATED | INCARNATE | GIST | AGONIZED | IMPLACABLY |

Death of a Salesman Vocabulary

| MERCURIAL | COMRADESHIP | STRIVING | INSINUATES | OVEREMPHASIZE |
|---|---|---|---|---|
| TREPIDATION | AVIDLY | PHILANDERING | SOLIDIFIED | ANXIOUSLY |
| SUBDUED | CLINCHES | FREE SPACE | IMPLACABLY | AGONIZED |
| GIST | INCARNATE | IMITATED | IDEALIST | CONTEMPTUOUS |
| CANDIDLY | REMISS | INTENT | DICTATION | LIABLE |

## Death of a Salesman Vocabulary

| OVERSTRUNG | CANDIDLY | RAUCOUS | TREPIDATION | LACONIC |
|---|---|---|---|---|
| SENSUOUS | INTENT | LIABLE | SOLIDIFIED | IMPLACABLY |
| DICTATION | PHILANDERING | FREE SPACE | IDEALIST | INSINUATES |
| MERCURIAL | SOLITARY | OVEREMPHASIZE | AGONIZED | CLINCHES |
| INCIPIENT | INCARNATE | REMISS | INCREDULOUSLY | IMITATED |

## Death of a Salesman Vocabulary

| CONTEMPTUOUS | FALTERS | STRIVING | DISPEL | ANXIOUSLY |
|---|---|---|---|---|
| OMINOUSLY | ENTHRALLED | AGITATION | BEFUDDLED | AVIDLY |
| GIST | SENTIMENT | FREE SPACE | IMITATED | INCREDULOUSLY |
| REMISS | INCARNATE | INCIPIENT | CLINCHES | AGONIZED |
| OVEREMPHASIZE | SOLITARY | MERCURIAL | INSINUATES | IDEALIST |

Death of a Salesman Vocabulary

| INCREDULOUSLY | LACONIC | CONTEMPTUOUS | ANXIOUSLY | AVIDLY |
|---|---|---|---|---|
| DICTATION | AGITATION | CLINCHES | SOLITARY | FALTERS |
| LIABLE | DISPEL | FREE SPACE | CANDIDLY | OVERSTRUNG |
| SUBDUED | IDEALIST | RAUCOUS | GIST | SENTIMENT |
| IMPLACABLY | INCIPIENT | INCARNATE | TREPIDATION | PHILANDERING |

Death of a Salesman Vocabulary

| COMRADESHIP | STRIVING | INTENT | OMINOUSLY | MERCURIAL |
|---|---|---|---|---|
| OVEREMPHASIZE | IMITATED | SENSUOUS | AGONIZED | INSINUATES |
| BEFUDDLED | ENTHRALLED | FREE SPACE | PHILANDERING | TREPIDATION |
| INCARNATE | INCIPIENT | IMPLACABLY | SENTIMENT | GIST |
| RAUCOUS | IDEALIST | SUBDUED | OVERSTRUNG | CANDIDLY |

## Death of a Salesman Vocabulary

| COMRADESHIP | SOLIDIFIED | STRIVING | CANDIDLY | GIST |
|---|---|---|---|---|
| SUBDUED | PHILANDERING | BEFUDDLED | INCARNATE | SENSUOUS |
| ANXIOUSLY | INCIPIENT | FREE SPACE | DICTATION | INSINUATES |
| MERCURIAL | INCREDULOUSLY | IDEALIST | SENTIMENT | TREPIDATION |
| OVERSTRUNG | AGONIZED | OMINOUSLY | REMISS | CONTEMPTUOUS |

## Death of a Salesman Vocabulary

| CLINCHES | SOLITARY | AVIDLY | DISPEL | IMPLACABLY |
|---|---|---|---|---|
| LACONIC | FALTERS | LIABLE | INTENT | OVEREMPHASIZE |
| AGITATION | ENTHRALLED | FREE SPACE | CONTEMPTUOUS | REMISS |
| OMINOUSLY | AGONIZED | OVERSTRUNG | TREPIDATION | SENTIMENT |
| IDEALIST | INCREDULOUSLY | MERCURIAL | INSINUATES | DICTATION |

## Death of a Salesman Vocabulary

| SENTIMENT | IMPLACABLY | INCIPIENT | INCREDULOUSLY | DICTATION |
|---|---|---|---|---|
| PHILANDERING | ANXIOUSLY | SUBDUED | SOLIDIFIED | OVEREMPHASIZE |
| IMITATED | TREPIDATION | FREE SPACE | SENSUOUS | BEFUDDLED |
| LIABLE | COMRADESHIP | ENTHRALLED | AGITATION | MERCURIAL |
| CLINCHES | IDEALIST | AVIDLY | LACONIC | CANDIDLY |

## Death of a Salesman Vocabulary

| FALTERS | STRIVING | INCARNATE | INTENT | SOLITARY |
|---|---|---|---|---|
| GIST | REMISS | AGONIZED | RAUCOUS | CONTEMPTUOUS |
| DISPEL | OMINOUSLY | FREE SPACE | CANDIDLY | LACONIC |
| AVIDLY | IDEALIST | CLINCHES | MERCURIAL | AGITATION |
| ENTHRALLED | COMRADESHIP | LIABLE | BEFUDDLED | SENSUOUS |

Death of a Salesman Vocabulary

| GIST | LIABLE | STRIVING | PHILANDERING | LACONIC |
|---|---|---|---|---|
| CONTEMPTUOUS | AGONIZED | SOLIDIFIED | AGITATION | COMRADESHIP |
| RAUCOUS | FALTERS | FREE SPACE | TREPIDATION | SUBDUED |
| REMISS | MERCURIAL | SOLITARY | INCIPIENT | SENSUOUS |
| OVERSTRUNG | INSINUATES | IMPLACABLY | ENTHRALLED | BEFUDDLED |

Death of a Salesman Vocabulary

| AVIDLY | ANXIOUSLY | DISPEL | IDEALIST | OVEREMPHASIZE |
|---|---|---|---|---|
| OMINOUSLY | SENTIMENT | IMITATED | CLINCHES | DICTATION |
| CANDIDLY | INCARNATE | FREE SPACE | BEFUDDLED | ENTHRALLED |
| IMPLACABLY | INSINUATES | OVERSTRUNG | SENSUOUS | INCIPIENT |
| SOLITARY | MERCURIAL | REMISS | SUBDUED | TREPIDATION |

Death of a Salesman Vocabulary

| BEFUDDLED | INTENT | AGITATION | AGONIZED | INCREDULOUSLY |
|---|---|---|---|---|
| IMITATED | IDEALIST | STRIVING | FALTERS | ENTHRALLED |
| SOLIDIFIED | SOLITARY | FREE SPACE | LIABLE | OMINOUSLY |
| INCARNATE | CANDIDLY | PHILANDERING | CLINCHES | OVERSTRUNG |
| DICTATION | IMPLACABLY | LACONIC | REMISS | GIST |

Death of a Salesman Vocabulary

| CONTEMPTUOUS | ANXIOUSLY | DISPEL | RAUCOUS | INSINUATES |
|---|---|---|---|---|
| MERCURIAL | TREPIDATION | SENTIMENT | OVEREMPHASIZE | SENSUOUS |
| INCIPIENT | COMRADESHIP | FREE SPACE | GIST | REMISS |
| LACONIC | IMPLACABLY | DICTATION | OVERSTRUNG | CLINCHES |
| PHILANDERING | CANDIDLY | INCARNATE | OMINOUSLY | LIABLE |

## Death of a Salesman Vocabulary

| MERCURIAL | AGONIZED | INCREDULOUSLY | REMISS | CLINCHES |
|---|---|---|---|---|
| LACONIC | OVEREMPHASIZE | STRIVING | INTENT | LIABLE |
| SENTIMENT | CONTEMPTUOUS | FREE SPACE | IMITATED | RAUCOUS |
| SOLITARY | CANDIDLY | DISPEL | AVIDLY | COMRADESHIP |
| OMINOUSLY | INCIPIENT | AGITATION | IMPLACABLY | INSINUATES |

## Death of a Salesman Vocabulary

| ENTHRALLED | INCARNATE | SOLIDIFIED | OVERSTRUNG | BEFUDDLED |
|---|---|---|---|---|
| IDEALIST | ANXIOUSLY | PHILANDERING | DICTATION | GIST |
| FALTERS | SUBDUED | FREE SPACE | INSINUATES | IMPLACABLY |
| AGITATION | INCIPIENT | OMINOUSLY | COMRADESHIP | AVIDLY |
| DISPEL | CANDIDLY | SOLITARY | RAUCOUS | IMITATED |

Death of a Salesman Vocabulary

| CONTEMPTUOUS | DICTATION | SENSUOUS | SOLITARY | LIABLE |
|---|---|---|---|---|
| RAUCOUS | FALTERS | COMRADESHIP | BEFUDDLED | LACONIC |
| INTENT | TREPIDATION | FREE SPACE | SUBDUED | IMPLACABLY |
| OMINOUSLY | AGITATION | MERCURIAL | CLINCHES | AVIDLY |
| INCREDULOUSLY | PHILANDERING | SOLIDIFIED | IDEALIST | GIST |

Death of a Salesman Vocabulary

| OVEREMPHASIZE | IMITATED | AGONIZED | STRIVING | REMISS |
|---|---|---|---|---|
| INCARNATE | DISPEL | INCIPIENT | ANXIOUSLY | OVERSTRUNG |
| INSINUATES | ENTHRALLED | FREE SPACE | GIST | IDEALIST |
| SOLIDIFIED | PHILANDERING | INCREDULOUSLY | AVIDLY | CLINCHES |
| MERCURIAL | AGITATION | OMINOUSLY | IMPLACABLY | SUBDUED |

Death of a Salesman Vocabulary

| DICTATION | INSINUATES | LACONIC | GIST | AVIDLY |
|---|---|---|---|---|
| INCARNATE | ENTHRALLED | INTENT | INCIPIENT | MERCURIAL |
| AGITATION | CANDIDLY | FREE SPACE | SOLITARY | STRIVING |
| TREPIDATION | IMITATED | IDEALIST | REMISS | SUBDUED |
| OMINOUSLY | SENTIMENT | SENSUOUS | OVERSTRUNG | FALTERS |

Death of a Salesman Vocabulary

| SOLIDIFIED | COMRADESHIP | INCREDULOUSLY | OVEREMPHASIZE | CLINCHES |
|---|---|---|---|---|
| RAUCOUS | LIABLE | ANXIOUSLY | BEFUDDLED | IMPLACABLY |
| CONTEMPTUOUS | PHILANDERING | FREE SPACE | FALTERS | OVERSTRUNG |
| SENSUOUS | SENTIMENT | OMINOUSLY | SUBDUED | REMISS |
| IDEALIST | IMITATED | TREPIDATION | STRIVING | SOLITARY |

Death of a Salesman Vocabulary

| AVIDLY | IDEALIST | FALTERS | IMITATED | MERCURIAL |
|---|---|---|---|---|
| ENTHRALLED | INTENT | IMPLACABLY | COMRADESHIP | STRIVING |
| RAUCOUS | INCARNATE | FREE SPACE | DISPEL | LACONIC |
| SOLITARY | INCIPIENT | OMINOUSLY | OVERSTRUNG | GIST |
| AGITATION | OVEREMPHASIZE | LIABLE | SENSUOUS | CONTEMPTUOUS |

Death of a Salesman Vocabulary

| CLINCHES | REMISS | ANXIOUSLY | DICTATION | SUBDUED |
|---|---|---|---|---|
| INCREDULOUSLY | INSINUATES | BEFUDDLED | CANDIDLY | AGONIZED |
| TREPIDATION | PHILANDERING | FREE SPACE | CONTEMPTUOUS | SENSUOUS |
| LIABLE | OVEREMPHASIZE | AGITATION | GIST | OVERSTRUNG |
| OMINOUSLY | INCIPIENT | SOLITARY | LACONIC | DISPEL |

Death of a Salesman Vocabulary

| OMINOUSLY | TREPIDATION | INTENT | SENSUOUS | AGITATION |
|---|---|---|---|---|
| MERCURIAL | ANXIOUSLY | INSINUATES | AVIDLY | INCIPIENT |
| SOLIDIFIED | COMRADESHIP | FREE SPACE | SOLITARY | LACONIC |
| CONTEMPTUOUS | OVEREMPHASIZE | STRIVING | GIST | FALTERS |
| SUBDUED | BEFUDDLED | OVERSTRUNG | INCARNATE | CLINCHES |

Death of a Salesman Vocabulary

| ENTHRALLED | DISPEL | LIABLE | RAUCOUS | INCREDULOUSLY |
|---|---|---|---|---|
| PHILANDERING | IDEALIST | DICTATION | REMISS | AGONIZED |
| IMITATED | CANDIDLY | FREE SPACE | CLINCHES | INCARNATE |
| OVERSTRUNG | BEFUDDLED | SUBDUED | FALTERS | GIST |
| STRIVING | OVEREMPHASIZE | CONTEMPTUOUS | LACONIC | SOLITARY |

Death of a Salesman Vocabulary

| OVERSTRUNG | SENSUOUS | ANXIOUSLY | DICTATION | FALTERS |
|---|---|---|---|---|
| IMPLACABLY | LACONIC | INCARNATE | SUBDUED | AVIDLY |
| STRIVING | RAUCOUS | FREE SPACE | CANDIDLY | REMISS |
| INTENT | COMRADESHIP | OMINOUSLY | INSINUATES | LIABLE |
| PHILANDERING | CLINCHES | AGITATION | AGONIZED | IDEALIST |

Death of a Salesman Vocabulary

| ENTHRALLED | CONTEMPTUOUS | BEFUDDLED | SENTIMENT | TREPIDATION |
|---|---|---|---|---|
| DISPEL | INCREDULOUSLY | INCIPIENT | SOLITARY | GIST |
| IMITATED | OVEREMPHASIZE | FREE SPACE | IDEALIST | AGONIZED |
| AGITATION | CLINCHES | PHILANDERING | LIABLE | INSINUATES |
| OMINOUSLY | COMRADESHIP | INTENT | REMISS | CANDIDLY |

## Death of a Salesman Vocabulary

| | | | | |
|---|---|---|---|---|
| SENSUOUS | IDEALIST | FALTERS | MERCURIAL | PHILANDERING |
| ENTHRALLED | LIABLE | OMINOUSLY | COMRADESHIP | AVIDLY |
| SOLIDIFIED | CLINCHES | FREE SPACE | INCARNATE | IMITATED |
| ANXIOUSLY | CONTEMPTUOUS | INCREDULOUSLY | LACONIC | DICTATION |
| INCIPIENT | SOLITARY | RAUCOUS | DISPEL | GIST |

## Death of a Salesman Vocabulary

| | | | | |
|---|---|---|---|---|
| AGONIZED | BEFUDDLED | SENTIMENT | SUBDUED | INSINUATES |
| TREPIDATION | REMISS | INTENT | CANDIDLY | AGITATION |
| IMPLACABLY | OVEREMPHASIZE | FREE SPACE | GIST | DISPEL |
| RAUCOUS | SOLITARY | INCIPIENT | DICTATION | LACONIC |
| INCREDULOUSLY | CONTEMPTUOUS | ANXIOUSLY | IMITATED | INCARNATE |

Death of a Salesman Vocabulary

| AGITATION | RAUCOUS | OMINOUSLY | INSINUATES | INCREDULOUSLY |
|---|---|---|---|---|
| CLINCHES | DICTATION | SUBDUED | SOLITARY | INCIPIENT |
| SENTIMENT | TREPIDATION | FREE SPACE | OVEREMPHASIZE | REMISS |
| AVIDLY | CONTEMPTUOUS | FALTERS | COMRADESHIP | SENSUOUS |
| AGONIZED | IMITATED | INTENT | LACONIC | PHILANDERING |

Death of a Salesman Vocabulary

| SOLIDIFIED | DISPEL | STRIVING | ENTHRALLED | OVERSTRUNG |
|---|---|---|---|---|
| MERCURIAL | IMPLACABLY | IDEALIST | CANDIDLY | INCARNATE |
| LIABLE | GIST | FREE SPACE | PHILANDERING | LACONIC |
| INTENT | IMITATED | AGONIZED | SENSUOUS | COMRADESHIP |
| FALTERS | CONTEMPTUOUS | AVIDLY | REMISS | OVEREMPHASIZE |

Death of a Salesman Vocabulary

| DISPEL | CLINCHES | INCREDULOUSLY | RAUCOUS | SOLIDIFIED |
|---|---|---|---|---|
| CONTEMPTUOUS | INSINUATES | OVERSTRUNG | ENTHRALLED | REMISS |
| CANDIDLY | OVEREMPHASIZE | FREE SPACE | AVIDLY | LACONIC |
| INTENT | AGITATION | ANXIOUSLY | IMPLACABLY | INCARNATE |
| IMITATED | SENSUOUS | FALTERS | SENTIMENT | PHILANDERING |

Death of a Salesman Vocabulary

| DICTATION | OMINOUSLY | LIABLE | TREPIDATION | AGONIZED |
|---|---|---|---|---|
| BEFUDDLED | GIST | SUBDUED | SOLITARY | COMRADESHIP |
| IDEALIST | INCIPIENT | FREE SPACE | PHILANDERING | SENTIMENT |
| FALTERS | SENSUOUS | IMITATED | INCARNATE | IMPLACABLY |
| ANXIOUSLY | AGITATION | INTENT | LACONIC | AVIDLY |

www.ingramcontent.com/pod-product-compliance
Lightning Source LLC
Chambersburg PA
CBHW081456070526
44586CB00019B/2384